Advance Praise

"The writing in *Natural Kill[...]* only the voice of a survivor [...] Lye recaptures the state of grace [...] darkest moments. She then brings us close to the absurdity and wonder of childbirth. In succinct and addictive and generous prose she details the perils and miracles of living in a human body, on the days when it is out to kill us and those when it is making a whole other life inside us."

—Heather O'Neill, author of *The Lonely Hearts Hotel* and *Lullabies for Little Criminals*

"Never have I read a more moving book on the fragile filament of life, the bond between people who love one another and struggle to find the words to express that love. The words are here, so wise and specific and drawn from the inward part. Harriet Alida Lye has no truck with fantasy or faith or folderol. She is a star witness to the bloom of life that surrounds death, and her work demands access to our unsentimental hearts."

—Michael Winter, author of *Into the Blizzard*

"*Natural Killer* is less a cancer memoir (though it is that) as a wise and heart-affirming reflection on the ties that bind us to one another: on motherhood but also daughterhood, control and surrender, and the body's limit experiences.

Harriet Alida Lye brilliantly weaves her materials together, from firsthand memories to medical records, scenes of the body ravaged and scenes of the body creating, in a truly original work of autobiography."

—Lauren Elkin, author of *Flâneuse: Women Walk the City in Paris, New York, Tokyo, Venice, and London*

"*Natural Killer* is a breathtaking memoir full of clarity, courage, and wisdom. In opening up her transition from child to mother, Harriet Alida Lye shows how fear and love can become unifying forces in a body that both takes and gives life. This story will stay with me for a long time."

—Claire Cameron, author of *The Last Neanderthal*

"A gripping memoir, told in an honest unassuming way that is inspiring and heartbreaking at the same time, and leaves you with renewed gratitude for life. I cried, I laughed, and I ached. The way Harriet weaves in her parents' perspective gave me goosebumps as a mother. I read this book in one night!"

—Samra Zafar, author of *A Good Wife*

"What a rare thing to read a book that makes you pause in reflection on nearly every page. *Natural Killer* is a remarkable story of an inspiring family that is both heartbreaking and hopeful. Harriet Alida Lye's writing, intimate and subtle, asks profound questions about life, death, hope, and trust that

Natural Killer

a memoir

Harriet Alida Lye

McClelland & Stewart

McClelland & Stewart and colophon are registered trademarks of
Penguin Random House Canada Limited.

Library and Archives Canada Cataloguing in Publication data is available upon request.
ISBN: 978-0-7710-4923-1
eBook ISBN: 978-0-7710-4924-8

Notes: while this is a work of non-fiction, it is also a work of memory.

The version of *Alcestis* quoted from was translated and adapted by Ted Hughes
(Farrar, Straus and Giroux, 1999).

Names of patients and medical staff have been changed.

Cover watercolour by Five Seventeen and Youn Joung Kim
Watercolour is based on an image of natural killer cell leukemia, courtesy of
Leibniz Institute, DSMZ-German Collection of Microorganisms and Cell Cultures GmbH.
Cell line: KHYG-1, DSMZ no.: ACC 725.

Typeset in Adobe Garamond Pro by M&S, Toronto
Emoji One [CC BY-SA 4.0 (https://creativecommons.org/licenses/by-sa/4.0)]

Printed and bound in the USA

McClelland & Stewart,
a division of Penguin Random House Canada Limited,
a Penguin Random House Company
www.penguinrandomhouse.ca

1   2   3   4   5   24   23   22   21   20

Penguin
Random House
McCLELLAND & STEWART

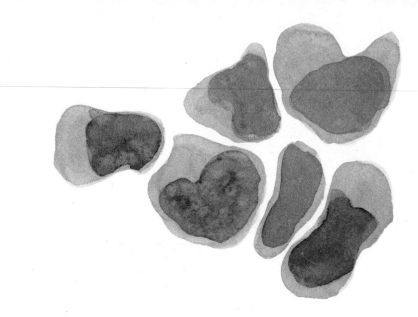

ALSO BY HARRIET ALIDA LYE

The Honey Farm

made me grateful to have spent time in her beautiful mind. This work, crafted so thoughtfully, will stay with me for a very long time."

—Ashley Audrain, author of *The Push*

"Harriet Alida Lye takes the enormous cruelty of indiscriminate disease and creates something truly beautiful and deeply moving. A book about the terror of death that is brimming with the warmth and vibrancy of life."

—Stacey May Fowles, author of *Baseball Life Advice*

"In this generous book, Harriet Alida Lye opens up her life—and her body—to us. She guides us through the peaks and nadirs of human experience with her sensuous prose, her keen eye for the beauty that exists even in the terrible moments, and, above all, her boundless, fierce love."

—Anna Maxymiw, author of *Dirty Work*

"Everything about this book is exceptional: the writing, the potency of its images, the portrayal of two lives linked across time, the writer herself. I cannot recommend this enough."

—Nafkote Tamirat, author of *The Parking Lot Attendant*

To my parents.

"Natural Killer Leukemia is the rarest
and worst malignancy."

INTERNATIONAL MEDICAL CASE REPORTS JOURNAL

"I have tried in my way to be free"

LEONARD COHEN

○

I got a bad cold in March and it never properly went away. It was 2002: I was in grade nine, and on March Break vacation with my parents in Niagara Falls. In the hotel swimming pool, I felt as though I was dissolving. As though I'd already disappeared. I could see people, flesh all around me, and I could feel the tepid chlorinated water on my skin, but I had the distinct feeling that I was no longer there, that these observations were coming from an objective, all-seeing place. I don't mean this spiritually—it felt factual. Like I'd forgotten I was alive.

I was in my first year in the drama program at a performing arts high school in suburban Toronto, and for the end-of-year play, I was cast as one of three girls playing the titular Queen in Euripedes's *Alcestis*. Our teacher, the director, had chosen to have the actors who played Alcestis also play the part of Death.

"When I awake in the body of Alcestis," I would say as

Death, "she dies," and then I'd pull back the hood of my black cloak and stand up as the self-sacrificing Queen.

Do you know the story? Beloved King Admetos is destined to die but his servant, the god Apollo, negotiates with Death to have a substitute die instead of the King. But nobody in the entire kingdom agrees to take his place. Not even Admetos's elderly parents, "two walking cadavers," will die to let their young son live. Finally, his wife Alcestis volunteers. Admetos suddenly regrets his cowardice and says he's now willing to die if his wife can live, but by this point, her offer cannot be retracted. Alcestis is taken away by Death.

"A god is deciding this"—her stoic parting words to her husband—"not me."

By April, I was pale and tired and too thin. In the last weeks of rehearsal I kept coughing through my lines. Just before the show, I woke up with burst blood vessels in my eyes, which, within hours, had drained to become deep bruises. I looked like I'd been punched.

I remember looking at myself in my bedroom mirror, staring at these candy-coloured purple smears around my eyes. The colouring was dappled, not consistent. It was pretty, blurred as if by water. I patted heavy concealer over the bruises, but a purple glow still shone through. People at school thought I was trying a weird new eyeshadow technique and when I told them it was blood, their faces registered fear.

My mum took me to a walk-in clinic, where the doctor dismissed me. "Her platelets must be low," he said, not thinking it was important to figure out how low, or why the drop.

"Can we get her a blood test?" my mum asked. "Maybe she needs to change her diet?"

"I'm not giving her a blood test to see if she needs to eat more steak," he said. "You can feed her as you like."

In my school play, Alcestis was carried offstage to face her fate, but at the last minute, young Heracles came to the rescue. "I fought with the God of Death," the boy playing this role, my friend, would recite with warmth and mockery, explaining how he got me back from the grave. "I surprised him, and trapped his neck in a lock."

Since I played Alcestis as well as Death, I wore both a gauzy white dress and a gauzy black cloak. Alcestis was stoic, devoted. Death was acerbic, exasperated. Both accepted things for what they were—I suppose you could say both were resigned.

Following the script, I died and came back to life in every show. I napped during intermission one evening, missed some morning classes in order to sleep in and stay late for the show, but I refused to miss a single performance despite my increasing inability to stay awake.

My body continued to break down: the back of my mouth started bleeding from an abscess developing on my tonsils; I woke up in the night because my arms had fallen asleep and the pain of the pins and needles would startle me out of my dreams. Once, right before my fifteenth birthday, I peed the bed. I was so embarrassed having to tell my mum what had happened. At first, she didn't even believe me.

"What happened?" she asked.

"I don't know, nothing. It just happened."

"Should we go to the hospital? Let's go to the hospital."

"No," I said. "I'm sure it's fine."

After the final show, though, when my indefinable illness had dragged on for nine weeks, I finally had blood tests done at the same walk-in clinic. This time, seeing the pools of blood underneath my eyes, the doctor did not refuse us. My mum brought me, and I brought along the neighbour's kids I was babysitting, since the clinic closed before my job ended. Bringing people for whom I was responsible made me feel less afraid: I had to be brave for someone.

When the results came back several days later, we got a call. I heard the voice mail, and was confused. "But why do I have to go back in?" I asked my mum. "Why can't they just tell us over the phone?"

My mum did well to mask her panic. I know now that she must have been terrified, that she must have sensed something. I obviously did, too, but we each needed to pretend to be fine for the other.

"I'm sure it's fine," she said, echoing me. "They just need to see you in person." An explanation that was no explanation at all.

At this point, the whites of my eyes were again filled with blood—like an oil spill, the fresh red all over the white, not mixing—and the bruises underneath my eyes were swollen. My skin was pale and glowing, like paper held to a lamp, and the abscess in my throat made eating painful. (I remember craving a Chicken Caesar sandwich from Arby's that was being advertised on TV at the time, and a freshly squeezed orange juice. I've never liked orange juice, and months later, when I finally got around to eating one of those Arby's sandwiches, the lettuce was slippery, the bread stale, and the dressing tasted like preservatives: it was not my fantasy at all.)

My mum took me back to the clinic and the doctor just stood there, holding the sheet of blood counts in his hand, looking at me with his eyes full of the fear that comes from facing the unknown. "I think you should see a specialist," he said, hurried. "I called a hematologist up here, but they don't have any appointments for a few weeks . . ."

He said some numbers, but the numbers didn't mean anything to me. They were my counts of hemoglobin, platelets, neutrophils. Numbers that I would become very familiar with soon. On his paper, they were all practically at zero.

Did this mean I had no blood in my body? I didn't understand.

"I'll take her to Sick Kids," my mum said. And then: "Should I take her to Sick Kids?"

He nodded.

We left.

That line ran through my head incessantly: "When I awake in the body of Alcestis, she dies." I was the girl, and I was death; both elements were within me.

My family doctor is a sixty-something hippie who runs courses on how psychotropic drugs can aid with finding peace at the end of one's life. He is constantly urging me to meditate instead of take sleeping pills, and when I had a concussion from a car accident, his recommendation was that I try interpretive dance. "Just feel your feelings," he said.

I go to him when, at thirty, I find out I'm pregnant.

"What news!" he says, clearly emotional. He, more than anyone, knows what a shock this is. All the drugs I was given as a teenager, the doctors told me back then, meant conception would be unlikely, if not impossible.

Now, my doctor gently smiles and pushes away from his desk to recline in his seat and takes off his glasses. I see a shine in his eyes, not quite tears.

With his words, he remains neutral. "Is this good news?" I love the generosity of his openness and feel grateful to him in the present as well as in some kind of alternate path, one in which my feelings about the pregnancy were different, and I didn't consider it to be good news. When I tell him that yes, it is good news, that my partner, Cal, and I are surprised but excited about, he smiles and sits back in his chair, putting his feet on the desk.

"What your body is doing now is completely magical," he says. "Not even science can explain it. Neurons are firing, eyeballs are growing, nerves will extend and then somehow miraculously land on all the right spots. Know that even if this baby does not get born, as miscarriage is fairly common, it is alive within you right now and you are holding this life."

I wonder if he would have been so forthright with a different patient. If it would have been necessary to bring death into the conversation so early. In his way, from the beginning, my doctor is reminding me to accept death within life. The baby is not a baby yet: it is a becoming.

He asks me if I've told my mother, also his patient. "No," I say. "Not yet."

"She'll be thrilled." He knows her well.

"But it isn't really about her," I say.

"Yes it is," he says. "It's about you, but it's also about her."

In dying, Alcestis asks her husband to grant her one favour—"Only a small thing. / Nothing to equal what I have given you. / I think you love our children as I do. / Admetos, let them be masters / In their own house. Do you understand me?"

This is what I long held as true: all children are their own masters. In becoming a mother, my understanding of vocabulary changes. Before, the possessive pronoun mothers use for their children irritated me. This is my baby; the baby is *mine*. It seemed petulant and incorrect: a child belongs to itself. It is a limitation of language that we don't have a word that can encompass how it can be both—that a child can be her own as well as belonging to her parents—but "my child" no longer seems quite such an improper term now that I am growing a human myself. Now I have a new understanding that I am my parents' child, and that the sick girl belonged to them in a truth deeper than law or biology.

"If nothing else," my doctor adds, "in becoming a mother, you make her a grandmother."

○

My mum and I rushed home from the doctor's office to
get my dad and pack a suitcase. I don't remember how long
I thought I'd be gone for—I might have brought one change
of clothes and a toothbrush. I do remember picking out
a white t-shirt that some friends had bought me for my
fifteenth birthday a few weeks before, with red sleeves and
the word *Guess* emblazoned in blue and red beads, fine as fish
roe. *I want to have my friends around me*, I thought, so self-
aware it was as if scripted. I held the t-shirt up and felt, for
the only time, a melodramatic self-pity, thinking of myself as
"being sick" and "going to the hospital." When things aren't
serious, people can take an indulgent, almost shameful
pleasure in experiencing pain. When things are serious,
there's no time or room for the fabrication of feeling.

I was meant to work at the hair salon on my block that
evening, where I worked as a receptionist after school.
I stopped in to say I was sorry I wouldn't be able to make

my shift. The owner was completely understanding, of course, and gave me some advice: "If you end up having to stay overnight, ask for an Ativan. It'll take the edge off."

We must have been in the middle of rush-hour traffic down to the children's hospital in the city, but I just remember leaning my head against the car window, and then being there. A brick archway and glass doors. My dad went to park and my mum and I walked through the sliding doors.

A nurse, a man in dark blue scrubs, took one look at me and said: "Oncology?" I am sure that I could recognize this nurse even now; I could pick him out of a lineup. Not as he would be now, of course—he is frozen as he was then.

I had no idea what the word *oncology* meant, and it turns out my mum didn't know either, but she said, without hesitation, "Yes." Later, she told me that this instinct came from the sense that saying yes would get us into a private room, and she wanted me to have as much quiet as possible.

We arrived at the Hospital for Sick Children on the Friday afternoon of the Victoria Day long weekend, and I did get a private room. It mattered that it was a long weekend because most of the procedure rooms were closed, which meant that I was given a three-day window of freedom. Maybe *freedom* isn't the right word here, since I was already embedded within a system, within a protocol, within a building, that I would be confined to for many months to come. But it was a limbo where we knew something was wrong, but not how wrong.

My room in the ER was windowless. I asked for Ativan, and was given it. I slept at odd hours, at all hours; I did not leave the room until Sunday. The hallway scared me; it felt like I could get lost out there. There were stretchers and blood, hushed voices and loud voices, babies screaming and adults crying. There were no windows anywhere except for the sliding glass doors on street level, and being in there felt like being in a bunker. Later, when I was brought up to different wings for tests, it was through a cargo elevator, not the main elevators in the glassy atrium. The whole ER wing seemed like a spatial, logistical impossibility—I never could place it within the architecture of the hospital.

After a few hours had gone by and I'd already been pricked for blood a dozen times, I was given an IV; the demand for blood exceeded my veins' ability to freely supply it. The IV went into the top of my left forearm, wrapped in gauze, and I could feel it all the time. In order to keep the vein open, a bag of saline hung from the swan's neck of a metal pole, and when the nurses needed to take blood, they would remove the tubing, seal off the saline, insert a needle into the rubber cap connecting to the pipe in my arm, and draw my blood into a syringe. If they didn't give me warning when this was going on and I happened to see my own blood, I'd either cry or scream.

Over the course of the weekend I answered the same questions to so many different cycles of doctors, but eventually, the doctors started becoming more consistent.

When it became clear a certain specialist wasn't needed, I suppose, they could do away with them. The ones who introduced themselves as hematologists and oncologists ended up being the ones who remained.

By Sunday morning I was in a room in a general wing on the sixth floor, with windows and a clearer view of the lay of the land. That afternoon, some friends and neighbours came down from our cul-de-sac in Richmond Hill, a suburb north of Toronto, with cake and cookies. It was my dad's birthday that day, and the treats doubled as "Happy Birthday" for my dad and "Get Well Soon" for me. This was back when such well-wishes were customary; back when it was still expected that I might get well soon.

There's one photo from that day, and I'm in my bed, eyes half closed, looking at the photographer—it must be my mother, as she's not in the photo. It's clearly a candid picture: nobody is looking at the camera except me, and I'm in the middle of saying something. My aunt is smiling, arms crossed, next to the neighbours from across the street. Two friends have their backs to the camera, their shiny brown ponytails pouring out of the frame. Another friend is standing in the doorway next to my dad. Everyone in the room is looking at my IV, and all the tubes behind my head, except for my dad. My dad is the only one looking at me. Our mouths are both slightly open; perhaps we're talking to each other. He's wearing a red plaid shirt and has a white paper badge affixed to his pocket that says PARENT.

On my right, there's a boxy grey computer on a huge wheeling cabinet, probably brought in so I could check the Hotmail account I hardly ever used. The screen saver on the computer is a black-and-white Anne Geddes photograph of two babies dressed as cherubs.

I'm sitting at the end of the cot, one leg flung over the metal barricade at the bottom, the other hanging off the side. A slipper is lost underneath the bed; my blankie and my lilac-coloured teddy bear, Lilac, are smushed between the pillows. I'm wearing a purple hospital gown and white sweatpants, my long dark hair tied up in a messy bun. The arm with the IV is propped on a plastic rectangle, taped into the package like a splint. This is so that the tubing won't bend.

My eyes—I have looked at this photograph so many times and only just now zoomed in on my eyes—are distant and disenchanted. The bruises beneath have faded a little— they're the size of fingerprints—but my right eyeball is, like a glass of Welch's grape juice, half-full of dark, bright blood.

2002-05-24, 17:05

Nature of illness: Unusual blood work
Place of accident: Not an accident
Brought to hospital by: Both parents
Triage classification: Urgent Team A

Asked by Onc. to assess for admission.

15 y/o female, awake, alert, pale, thin, with pancytopenia and unwell since March; tonsillitis; fever on and off; night sweats + weight loss

○

When some preliminary results had come in, we were told that it could be one of three things: mono, aplastic anemia, or leukemia. If it was leukemia, they said it was probably one of two types: ALL—acute lymphocytic leukemia—or acute myeloid leukemia: AML. The first one was more common among children—at fifteen, I was still a child— and had a longer treatment protocol, but a much higher survival rate. At the time, the survival rate was around 90 per cent, and the treatment lasted for two years. Most of that time was as an outpatient, though, with the children able to live at home. Kids with ALL are on steroids for a large part of their treatment. These kids had been pointed out to me on the ward: swollen toddlers with huge cheeks and thinning hair sticking out of their scalps like electrocuted baby chicks.

The doctors talked less about AML in that brief pre-diagnosis period, focusing instead on the option with the higher survival rate. I did know that the treatment for AML was shorter, and much more intense. Over time, I gleaned that the remission rate was around 50 per cent, but the relapse rate was high. Googling it now, I've learned that the five-year survival rate in 2002 was less than 10 per cent.

I'd never heard of aplastic anemia, so I privately decided it could not be that. And while I had a feeling I wouldn't be this deep into a long weekend in the Hospital for Sick Children if it was just mono, I gave myself a fifty-fifty chance between mono and cancer.

Nobody talked about Natural Killer yet. That wasn't on the table.

With the long-weekend limbo over, I was booked into a procedure room and put under anaesthetic for a spinal tap and a bone marrow aspirate. Needles were inserted into the liquid inside of my spine and in the space between my hips where stem cells grow. I was told there would be an ache for a few days afterwards, but there was so much else going on that I didn't notice any aching there.

On Monday, the day after my dad's birthday, many of the doctors I recognized from Emergency filed into my room. There were five, maybe six doctors encircling my bed, pressed up against the walls, as far away from me as possible.

"It looks like cancer," they said.

I don't remember if I said this out loud, but my thought was: "It looks like cancer, or it is cancer?"

(When I ask my dad now, he says, "Oh, you said it out

loud. You were very astute, actually—you spoke before your mum or I even had time to have a thought.")

The doctors said they were still figuring out exactly what kind of cancer it was.

I asked how long the treatment would last.

"Around six months."

So, I realized, it was the worse cancer.

"Will I be in the hospital for that whole time?"

"You might be able to go home for a few days at a time, but it's likely you'll be here for most of that, yes."

Six months, I thought. *Fine. After six months, I'll be fine.*

I immediately framed the situation so that my only problem was time.

The doctors asked if there were any more questions. I remember silence. I remember looking at my feet under the sheets, the shape of them making ghost mountains, and the feeling of being looked at.

Though I'd had what seemed like litres of blood removed for tests over the previous few days, the presence of the cancer was so diffused in the samples they'd taken that it was not possible to form an accurate diagnosis. Many people have aberrant cancer cells floating in their blood that will naturally disappear before developing into an illness. Once they obtained those samples of my bone marrow, however—the tissue that produces blood cells— they saw that it was nearly 100 per cent cancerous. If treatment didn't start within three days, they told us,

I would die. If I had come to the hospital three days later, I would not have lived.

The doctors left. I fell asleep, and ate leftover cake when I woke up.

∞

When I was twenty, I tried to write a novel about my experience. From the beginning, it was the story of a fifteen-year-old girl who got sick, then died. I spent eight years working out the rest of the story, all of the accompanying surges of narrative, but that part always remained the same. The girl died, like I'd been supposed to die.

I was telling a new friend about the novel I'd spent so long working on, and like many others, she asked why the protagonist died. I always responded with the same thing: Beatrice dies because I didn't, but was supposed to. Because so many people die. Because that's life.

But this friend asked a question that nobody else had: "Did you *want* to die?"

Or maybe she said it like this: "Did *you* want to die?"

Either way, the answer has always been obvious to me. No.

That was the first time I considered changing the ending.

Nurse's notes in the progress report from the diagnosis:

Parents + Harriet have a realistic view of treatment. They
asked appropriate questions and responded appropriately.
Emotional support ++ offered + required. Overall Harriet
appears to be a bright, intelligent teenager with relevant
concerns and issues. Much support is needed.

Doctor's notes in the progress report from the diagnosis:

~ 1400-1430hrs, parent + PT told results of BMA. Leukemia.
Awaiting confirmation of type. Shock, reaction.

Note: Cytometry results not consistent with diagnostic of AML.

Abridged psychology report from after the diagnosis:

When we first met Harriet, she was lying down in bed and appeared visibly tired. Harriet indicated that at that point she did not want to participate in any preliminary discussions about psychological consultations and suggested that it is best if we talk with her parents. Since Harriet's mother was not present, we asked Mr. Lye to talk privately about his concerns regarding Harriet and his family's psychological adjustment. Mr. Lye stated that after Harriet found out about her diagnosis, she cried for about half an hour and then dealt with it "head on." At the conclusion of the session, we went back to Harriet's room.

Harriet was anticipating intake of heavily sedating medication and she did not want to have any discussions about psychology at that point. She only asked that her father stay by her side when she is receiving the medication.

○

After the diagnosis I was immediately moved up to the eighth floor—the cancer ward. I didn't have time to dwell on what this meant. To *have* cancer. To *be* cancerous. Actually, I had nothing but time, but time did not belong to me. I did not *have* time.

My room had a window with a ledge where I could sit, craning my neck around the brick wall directly opposite to look down at the street. I could see people walking to work, to the subway, to get coffee. I couldn't believe that, for so much of the world, life was continuing as normal.

The first round of chemo had to begin right away, before my permanent IV had been inserted, and the drugs burned the narrow veins in my arm. It hurt so much that, sometimes, I had to be held down.

The nurse delivering one of the treatments wore a lead apron, like you wear when getting your mouth X-rayed at the dentist. Because of the risk of exposure to the chemicals, nobody else was allowed to be in the room with me when those drugs were being administered. *So what is this doing to me?* I thought.

I was so sick and so tired that the only path I wore was from my cot to the bathroom, where I had to trundle my IV behind me and manoeuvre it into a corner in order to pee. I tried leaving the machine outside since it took up so much space, but I hated having the door open when someone was in the room. The bathroom was the only place where I had any sort of privacy at all, and even then, every time I peed I had to put a specially made plastic bucket into the toilet to capture the urine, which would then be tested by the nurses. They had to monitor how much liquid went in and how much came out; pH levels; whether there were any signs of infection. This, even more than my IV, made me feel like a body-machine.

I could get the IV temporarily disconnected in order to bathe—a nurse would have to come to sterilize the caps and seal them off with 3M tape—but the little pouch of tubes would permanently hang from my body, and getting them wet would risk infection, which would mean getting the IV inserted all over again. I was incredibly protective of it. At the time it felt like fear, but I wonder now if it wasn't something like pride.

One of the things everyone knows—and everyone asks about—is that people with cancer lose their hair. I was told that this would happen quickly, given the strength of drugs

I was being given. Because it was very hard not to get my IV wet, but also because I had little physical strength at that time, I needed help showering. I've never been the kind of person to be naked around my family, not even as a child, so I wore a t-shirt and underwear and sat in the bathtub as my mum stood behind me, holding the shower head low.

"It's too hot," I shouted. "Now it's too cold!" I hadn't bathed or brushed my hair in a long time, and my hair was beginning to form dreadlocks around my neck. I was terrified of brushing it; I didn't want to lose it. Once it was gone, I felt, it would be gone forever. "You're making it fall out!" I shrieked, seeing strands on the porcelain around me.

"That's normal," my mum said, trying to be calm though I could tell she was not finding this easy either. "Hair falls out when you shower!"

I frantically counted the strands and tried to determine whether the amount was in fact normal or whether, instead, the chemo was taking effect, but I didn't know what "normal" was in this place.

oo

When the shock of my pregnancy had settled, I felt
enormously porous to the world. Walking down the street,
I noticed people's cheeks pinking in the February wind.
There were plastic buckets of tulips outside the fruit market
at the corner—red, pink, orange, purple, yellow. I wanted
them all. I wanted to have them, to eat them, to *be* them.
I was super-living, living for two, larger than usual and my
eyes more open than they'd been the previous week.

Someone told me that to be a mother is to make a death,
because death is bound up in life, but this did not feel like
a revelation. I knew my body could create death. I'd never
trusted, was told to not even imagine, that it also had the
power, that magical banality, to create *life*.

HARRIET'S PATIENT ID: 1200174

To use laptop computer:
1) Plug in power adaptor
2) Turn on PC
3) password: childlife

Lower limit of red cells: 70-80
Platelets ~40
THEN THEY WILL TRY TO DO A TRANSFUSION

Thursday May 30th 3pm: Harriet's braces to come off b/c mouth sores

List of things to bring:
- hair elastics
- coat hangers
- phone cable

○

My cousin in England set up one of those old-school websites for me, with a forum and picture galleries and a visitor counter on the home page. I would update it myself sometimes, but it was more often my parents who wrote. It was a helpful way for them to deflect acquaintances who asked after me in the grocery store: "Just check the website," they would say, not wanting to talk about it any more than necessary.

At the recommendation of the medical staff, my parents kept a journal in which they could record, hour by hour, everything that happened every day so as to go back to it later to check for patterns, or side effects; or perhaps just to have a purpose, something to do when they were alone with their thoughts in my hospital room as I slept.

They started the journal on the eleventh day. It's a pale-green, spiral-bound notebook with yellow-and-red parrot tulips on the front, with disproportionally sized animals—a tiny turtle, a giant ladybug—among the foliage. The journal's original job was to sit beside the phone in the kitchen and receive messages; the first few pages were ripped out when it found its new purpose.

There's a pink Post-it Note sticking out about a quarter of the way through that doesn't seem to be flagging anything specific, some business cards of social workers and hospital teachers interspersed among the pages, and at the back is a table my dad made to keep track of my daily blood counts: white, red, platelets, and polymorphs/ neutrophils, the white blood cells most closely monitored during my treatment as they indicate whether or not the body is capable of fighting infection. Often the white blood cells were at less than one, so the neutrophils were untraceable. My mum bought a parrot puppet from the hospital gift shop that she called Polly, to celebrate, when the time came, the return of the polymorphs: "The polys are back, the polys are back!" the parrot would cry on behalf of my mother.

My parents took turns being with me, and writing in the notebook: everything that happened was documented. If an aunt or friend came to offer respite for an afternoon or evening, that person would take over the record-keeping. While the notebook started in earnest on June 4, I found notes my dad had gone back to write later on the last page of the book, annotating the major events of those first few days for the Official History, starting on his birthday.

SUN MAY 26

Awaiting Bone Marrow Aspirate. Negative for Mono in all tests so far.

MON 27

Bone Marrow Tests. News of Leukemia, in 7C all together. Shock, then regaining composure.

TUE 28

Awaiting tests to determine ALL or AML. 4pm diagnosis of AML. Also heart echo.

My dad's authorship over these days is so simple, certain, and nuanced. That he wrote "Shock, then regaining composure." It echoes the doctor's progress report—*Shock, reaction.*—which my dad would definitely not have seen. Whom did he write that for? How does one determine "composure"? Did we all really regain our composure so quickly? Once that announcement was made, was it never to be lost again?

Also: "all together." The three of us, our tiny family unit. And his noting, for the record, our small, retroactive hope that it would be ALL—the one with a higher survival rate—and how that hope shattered at precisely four p.m.

∞

My parents have a home video of my ninth birthday party where they ask all my toothy nine-year-old friends what they want to be when they grow up. A lot of dance teachers, a lot of lawyers.

When it comes to me, I think for five full seconds (I've timed it on the video), rolling my tongue around behind my lips. Then I mumble something to my mum, almost privately.

"Louder, Harriet," she says. "Tell us—what do you want to be when you grow up?"

My dark hair is tied in a low ponytail and I'm wearing stick-on pearly earrings. I repeat my answer, this time a little louder: "an artist." Then I look down at the table, smile, and pick up my juice box.

On camera, looking at myself now, I think I look equal parts bashful and pleased. Like I'd reached the right conclusion, one I was privately thrilled about, but one that I knew had embarrassing connotations.

At this point, was the cancer already lying in wait?

O

My friends came to visit and said I looked beautiful, more beautiful than usual. I had been wearing the same pyjamas for a week, my hair was so dirty it was dreadlocking again, and I had no need or desire to wear any makeup. I obviously thought they were trying to be nice, but the tone of their voices—not just surprised but skeptical, as though I could somehow be lying about how sick I was—confused me. As the chemo was burning through my blood, I can see in photographs that a sense of calm had come across my expression. I do remember feeling a certain purity at that time—an unquestioning devotion to my being there, to surrendering my body to the medical system. My whole purpose was to get well. I didn't have to do anything else.

Looking at the photos now, I think I see what they might be talking about. It's when flowers are closest to death that they are in their fullest bloom.

○

The walls of the eighth-floor bedrooms were peach and green, and there was a small, uncomfortable "sofa" that turned into a bed. My parents took turns sleeping there every night—they called it the Changing of the Guard. One of them was always with me, the other one alone at home.

The bedroom I stayed in quickly filled with photographs and decorations. My aunt gave my classmates a bag full of disposable cameras and told them to document their days, the ordinary days I'd been living up until a few days before. Posing in front of hallway lockers, running across the soccer field, bright flashes on pale faces in the dark drama room. The printed photos were tacked up on my wall, on all the walls of every room I was moved to. I had three boxes of decorations that we'd lug around, filled with yellow streamers and drawings by my young cousins.

My bed was on wheels and had metal barricades that could be raised or lowered, and a button to bring the back up into a seated position. I tried not to think about the fact that my bed was also a stretcher. There was another red button right next to the bed, too, which functioned like the buttons on airplanes to request a flight attendant. The button sent a page to the nurses' station, the nucleus in the centre of the ward from which the various corridors branched out.

A TV hung from the ceiling, and at first, I was excited to watch all the daytime television that being at school normally precluded. *Dawson's Creek*, *The Price is Right*, cartoons. I quickly grew bored with all that, though, and stopped watching TV after a week or so.

Friends would ask how I spent my days. They couldn't fathom how time passed for me, and it's hard to say, now; it was hard to say then. But scanning through the journal, it strikes me that there's something happening every twenty minutes or so, at least. Doctors came to examine me or prescribe medications; pharmacists came to explain side effects of medications; nurses came to take my vitals and give me medications and transfusions. Visitors were often coming by—friends, family, people we got to know in the hospital. I was sent to get ultrasounds or X-rays or some other kind of test almost every day, too, and that could take hours: getting ready, being transported there, waiting for the test, having the test performed, then waiting for a transport worker to bring me back. I was always being given food, always trying to sleep. The in-house clown, Posy, came to visit weekly. She didn't talk, which I liked.

On the back of one of the lunch menus, which came on long, narrow parchment-style paper with perforated, hole-punched edges, my dad wrote a list of things I could do in the months that extended before me.

THINGS TO DO IN HOSPITAL
1. Watch TV
2. Learn a new language (eg Spanish, Italian, German, Latin) from tapes, books & people
3. Learn to knit (to make scarves etc for friends)
4. Write stories, or plays, or essays, songs, just for fun & to let stuff out (like Dumbledore's Pensieve)
5. Learn to play chess, or Mahjong, or ?
6. Read interesting books, for fun & to satisfy curiosity
7. Use hospital library for medical research
8. Connect with other people in this hospital, or others, for mutual support
9. Develop drawing & painting skills (why not)
10. Sleep (of course)
11. Exercise
12. Write letters to people, everyone loves to get mail
13. Make your own Individual Education Plan for the first part of grade 10, after checking resources and curriculum on the web
14. Explore the whole hospital
15. Learn a new musical instrument (eg guitar)
16. + LOTS, LOTS MORE

There is hope in a list, and such an urgent hope in this one. *Live, Harriet, do all of these things, make it through your time here, live, please live, and do lots, lots more.* Why not. Of course.

○

The surgery to insert the central line happened on the eleventh day—June 4. As I said, this was the first day of the journal.

A central line is a "central venous catheter" inserted into a large vein—mine was the jugular—to facilitate regular and easy access to the bloodstream. It's like a port into the body. We had been told that the procedure was fairly dangerous, as general anaesthetic and a full-on surgery are riskier for people with compromised immunity.

The insertion of a central line felt like admitting something I'd been trying to keep at the margins, though I was assured that it was just protocol. The nurses reminded me that the peripheral ivs in my forearms were annoying and painful to replace, and the chemo burned through the veins so quickly that they needed to find new veins regularly, sometimes many times a day.

My mother's writing in the notebook:

Central line scheduled today. Needed platelets & packed
red cells—A.M. platelets still not up to 100 (66) but will be
proceeding at 1pm.

1:50 Dr. Mavrou re. Central Line

Dr Ross—anaesthesiologist? Good name for H's first born!

3:15 Dr Mavrou says H is fine with blood counts now! Good
to go ☺

Lying on my back, bright lights spotlighting my body, the
masked face of the anaesthesiologist floating directly above
my face.

"Count backwards from ten," Dr. Ross said.

I doubted him. I felt defiant; if I wanted to stay awake,
I would.

I was gone by eight.

Then, in my father's hand:

4:15 in recovery room, after Double Lumen line inserted. No
problems.

6pm chicken fingers and fries.

When I woke up in the recovery room in my own bed
(another reminder that my bed was just a stretcher that
could be moved around the hospital), my body felt different.
I was still wearing the same hospital gown and sweatpants,
but my body didn't feel quite like mine.

Looking down, I could see tubes coming out of my chest

that were about as long as drinking straws. The same matte white, too. The knot of plastic tubing lifted the chalk-white flesh, making my skin look remarkably like rubber. Blood scabbed around the point of entry, covered with a thin patch of clear medical tape. At the bottom end of the white-straw part, clear plastic IV tubes twisted on to attach to the pump, and to any bag of fluid that needed to be hung from the pole. I assumed that they—the doctors, or the designers of the device—kept it opaque up high because of how blood has the tendency to ooze out. An important rule: never let patients see their own insides.

In the bathroom, I lifted my hospital gown and saw brown lines drawn on my skin. Iodine lines, to sterilize— and to demarcate where the veins were? I don't know. Maybe. I was never told. I never asked; this was just my best guess.

I felt embarrassed. I felt violated. People had seen me naked. While I was unconscious, they had painted on my body.

Further evidence that I was theirs. Their patient, their subject. Nothing was mine anymore.

∞

Since I wasn't supposed to be alive, I wrote in a journal a year after being released from the hospital, *all of this is bonus time.*

○

I was surprised by how *loud* things were in the hospital.
My IV pump would beep, and when it wasn't beeping, it was
breathing: the sound of suction and liquids passing through
created a constant rhythmic accompaniment that sounded
almost human. While I had a door, nobody who worked in
the hospital ever knocked. Anyone could come and go, take
my blood, take my temperature, take my meal tray away;
they could even take me—down to a different floor for
a scan, to a different room for a tubing change.

Announcements came through the PA system from eight
a.m. to eight p.m., separate announcements from within
the unit and throughout the whole hospital. Doctors being
paged, nurses being sent to specific patients' rooms. The
patients were never mentioned by name, only by room
number. If I pressed the red button next to my bed, the
receptionist would call out: *Jen to room 24 please, Jen to
room 24.*

The one I heard most often was: *Keys to the desk please, keys to the desk.* The narcotics were kept under lock and key and there was only one key, held by one specific person each shift.

I asked a nurse what a narcotic was. "Morphine, codeine, cocaine . . . that kind of thing."

"You have cocaine here?" I'd heard of cocaine before, obviously, but from what I'd heard, I did not think it was the kind of thing that would be prescribed to kids with cancer. "What do you use it for?"

"When nosebleeds get really bad," the nurse started, then looked at me tentatively, wondering whether she'd said too much but realizing it was too late to stop now: "well, we can create a mixture using cocaine to paint into the nostrils—it constricts the blood vessels and can slow the bleeding."

The hospital-wide pages were reserved for more serious codes, which I quickly learned: yellow was for missing persons, blue was for heart attacks.

"Kids can have heart attacks?" I asked the nurse.
She nodded.

○

Harriet said "one good thing about being here is there are
no spiders!" Watched *Dirty Dancing* 'til midnight

The first round of chemotherapy lasted two weeks and
continued through the central line, so the drugs no longer
burned my veins; I couldn't feel anything through the
permanent IV. The symptoms were as you would expect. It
was so hard on me physically that I was able to elude the
emotional consequences.

I developed a fever partway through that first round and,
for reasons that everyone tried to keep from me, this was
a very bad thing. I did understand that fevers meant infection,
and with the chemotherapy knocking out my immune system,
any kind of infection caused concern since there was nothing
to fight it off. I reminded everyone, including the doctors and
nurses, to Purell their hands before coming into my room.

I lost nineteen pounds in those two weeks. The nutritionist, a tiny woman with giant curly hair, told me that to keep up with the weight loss I should eat as many Häagen-Dazs bars as possible and replace the milk in my cereal with cream. She asked what my cravings were.

"Blueberries," I said.

She laughed. "You need to want to eat, like, hamburgers and ice cream."

I had to be started on intravenous nutrition supplements. One huge bag of urine-coloured liquid, and one small bag of opaque white liquid. Vitamins, and fat. It was called total parenteral nutrition, or TPN. My nurses reminded me that this wasn't an excuse to stop eating, that I should still try to eat whatever I could, and that hopefully I could get off the liquid food soon. It was hard on the liver, they said, but I think it was probably harder on the spirit. Eating is more than sustenance. It's community, it's pleasure. (Like the neighbourhood meal plan a family friend organized for us. People signed up to take turns making all three of us dinner every single night, which gave us all such a strong sense of both community and pleasure, even if I couldn't eat.)

Friends came all the way downtown, about an hour by car or nearly three on public transit, and sometimes I was too sick to see them. My parents would say hello, then turn them away on my behalf. I didn't have the energy to feel guilty.

My friend who played Heracles—"I fought with the God of Death"—came to visit often. When I was well enough to see him, he'd ask if he could hug me.

I said no. "Germs."

Young Heracles bought me a four-foot-tall purple plastic gerbera daisy that was balanced in an iron frame. Later, a doctor on his rounds said, very seriously: "You know flowers aren't allowed, don't you?" My dad laughed until he had tears in his eyes.

○○

Cal and I met at the dog park in the spring, when we each got our puppies—my Fox, his Disco. Cal has Windex-blue eyes and, from the first time I talked to him, I could tell he was shy but self-assured. Fox and Disco loved each other immediately and fervently, the kind of love that comes only from animal instinct. They'd play under the picnic table in the park to hide from the desert-like summer sun, gently gnawing each other's mouths.

Cal had bought an old camper van before we'd met, and on our first real date he told me he planned to quit his job and spend a summer driving first east, then west. I told him I had the framework of a book tour building up that would take me east, then south, and there was no reason I couldn't also go west.

It was one of those plans made half jokingly, after a few drinks, but on that first date, we decided to merge itineraries. Half joke, half promise. The van became a stand-in for commitment: when we talked about this trip, we were placing signposts into our future, saying we wanted to be together for at least as long as the trip would last.

We took action to make the metaphor more concrete. He bought a solar panel. I bought fairy lights.

More than once, as we lay in bed falling asleep, I'd ask in a panic: "Are you sure you want to do this with me? Your original plan was to go alone."

"That was before I met you," he'd say. "The plan changed." He's one of those people who says what he means and does what he says, which can be just as disarming as the opposite.

One thing we hadn't planned for when mapping out the trip, though, was that I'd be doing it during my second trimester. I found out I was pregnant on Valentine's Day, and neither one of us thought it was cause to change our summer plans.

Very early on I'd explained to him that if, somehow, I were ever to become pregnant, I wouldn't want to get an abortion. I never thought I'd be able to deny the opportunity for life to grow in my body, and Cal understood where I was coming from. This wasn't a plan to have a child, not at all; it was rather a plan of what to do in case that happened. And when that did happen, we went away to a cabin in the woods with our dogs to talk about it.

We walked across a lake of solid ice and let the dogs loose on the snowy island crowded with black pines. The pipes were frozen, so we brought a flat of water for drinking and peed in a bucket filled with kitty litter. The temperature inside the cottage was well below freezing, and the fire in the wood stove took three days to warm it up, by which time we put it out to head back home.

We didn't talk about it, then we talked around it, and then we talked about it, and decided that it felt like the decision had been made, and when it was put before us like that, we didn't want to undo it. This is perhaps an unromantic way of saying we wanted to have a baby together, but decisions made retroactively—maybe even any decisions at all—have a kind of contractual nature. There should be pragmatism as well as an animal instinct.

"Are you sure this is what you want?" I asked, again. "This wasn't your plan."

"I love you," Cal said, "and I don't think I could have known that this is what I wanted until now that it's already happening."

○

MONDAY JUNE 10

2:35 Dr D and Dr A come to see Harriet. Order chest x-ray.
   If fever lasts until tomorrow, amphotericin = anti-fungal.
   Ultrasound for spleen, liver, pancreas, and kidneys re.
   fungal work-up.

TUESDAY JUNE 11

6pm, starting amphotericin with Benadryl & Tylenol to
   counter potential side effects. If she starts shaking they
   will administer Demerol.

If she starts shaking, if she starts shaking.

The terrifying reality of *shaking* mitigated by the hope of
the conditional *if.* The *she,* their sick girl-child—I so rarely
felt like an object or like anyone's possession, but this is
a reminder that I was. The *starts,* as in: It will just be the
beginning.

THURSDAY JUNE 13

11:30am Harriet awakens

11:40am Harriet had a few grapes

1:30pm Harriet had some rest, put on her eye mask, turned
    off light

1:40pm IV beeping! Not much rest!

Some things that break my heart: My dad's use of the word
"awakens," as though I was a lady of leisure lounging in bed
all through the morning, and not a teenager with cancer
who'd been up all night with a fever. Ditto for "grapes."
I love him for granting me that.

○

The first time I left my room on my own feet, and not for any appointment, was on Friday, June 14. It was also the first time—and one of the very few times—that I wrote in the notebook myself:

>   4:50pm Walked (yeah! bit shaky though) down to get X-ray done. Back in 10 mins—very quick, no lineups!

At this point I had been in the hospital for twenty-two days, but already it seemed like it had been my whole life, and would continue to be my whole life.

The worst part was waking up and, for the briefest of moments, forgetting where I was.

∞

Going through stuff in my parents' basement, I find
a toolbox I used to carry from room to room in the hospital.
My parents were encouraged to give me spaces that could
be "private." The toolbox locked, but had a clear front.
Close enough.

I open the box and find art supplies I never used,
orange foam earplugs, and the business card of Posy the
clown. In the hospital, I'd started sleeping with earplugs to
muffle the constant cacophony of sound; I still sleep with
them every night. Like a child with a teddy bear, I can't sleep
without them. I always use the orange foam ones you squeeze
up small, insert into your ear, then let swell up to fill the dark
spaces. Seeing these fresh earplugs in the box, I pocket them
to use for later. There is also an email address on a pink
Post-it Note: *curlysue_baby14, Sofia (from the hospital).*

Sofia was my age and had osteosarcoma. We were introduced at Sick Kids. She was tall, like me, and soft-spoken,

and it felt like we would have been friends in the normal world, outside of the hospital, even had we not been pushed together by the nurses because of our proximity in age. When I was home between rounds of chemo, Sofia came over. At fifteen, we didn't say "come over to play," like when we were younger, but she didn't really come over to do anything in particular. I had a computer program where you could upload a picture of yourself and then put makeup and different hairstyles over your picture to give yourself a "makeover." We took pictures of each other and then did that, putting on more digitally-painted makeup than either of us would have ever worn, though giving ourselves not platinum bouffants or anything, but our own normal straight brown hair again.

A few months after that, Sofia died. Her funeral was held at a local mosque, in a field surrounded by encroaching subdivisions. My parents and I sat on carpets on the floor. I remember looking out at the grey sky, the light filtering through the darkened window beside me. I didn't believe that God was deciding any of this, and yet here we were. Nobody else had decided it, either.

I put down the toolbox and Google Sofia. I find a picture of her, short brown hair newly growing back, wide brown eyes, smiling in a khaki bucket hat at Camp Oochigeas, a camp for kids with cancer. The caption reads, "Sofia loves Camp!" In the present tense. There is a place in the world where Sofia still exists in the present tense.

The sadness I feel now is awakening a sadness I feel always, and I can't tell if it's pure or if it's selfish, an "it could have been me" sadness. Is that selfish, or is that human?

○

Midway through the first round of chemotherapy, the doctors met with my parents separately from me, and they also offered me my first opportunity at leaving the hospital. It's easy to see now how those two events were connected. Tactic: give them a carrot so they can handle the stick. These were professionals.

JUNE 18TH *(my dad's hand)*

9:40am Nurse Jenna has talked to Dr. D, and it looks like a short pass out is possible after the blood, which must be after the Vancomycin, so maybe 3:30-5:30 window. Will meet at 5:30pm today for HL, ML, DL + Drs.

10:15am Dr. L visited, some new results back, from flow cytometry and cytogenetics. There is a "marker" called CD56 that has been detected. Meeting is to discuss tactics. Bone Marrow Transplant looks like a good option for near term rather than later. "NK cell" leukemia may be involved.

That pre-meeting was the part to which I was not privy. If I had been, I would have asked what the letters N and K stood for.

> 12pm Vitals 37.0
> 12:40 Blood transfusion started
> 12:55 Vitals again. 36.8. All OK. Fluconazole tablets started again.
> 1:20 Harriet had a bath *("1/2" is added later, in my wobbly handwriting. I must have wanted it to be clear for the record that I did not wash my hair.)*
> 3:40–4:45 Freedom! All 3 of us walked south to Colony Hotel just by City Hall, for Iced Tea and Salad (Harriet), & Ploughman's Lunch (D & M shared) on the patio called Nathan's Backyard. Lovely interlude.
> **Harriet wished she could come here every day!—Mum

For the first time in nearly a month, for one hour and fifteen minutes, I was not connected to an IV. I didn't have to pull or push a machine alongside me. The tubes coming out of my upper right side were sterilized and wrapped up in gauze and made a little sausage underneath my t-shirt.

"Living in the moment" has become an industry, but for those seventy-five minutes, I did not consider the meeting that was scheduled for that afternoon. Maybe this is because I hadn't been briefed on what to expect, but I think it was because my senses were so overwhelmed. Red sun-shapes through closed eyelids. The trembling of the sidewalk when the subway rumbled below. Wind through the leaves on the thin, undernourished city trees.

It was freedom, as my dad said. A freedom aware of its constraints. And *interlude* was the perfect word there, too, for it means "between the acts." This was a brief moment, right before what the doctors explained what they expected would be the final act.

5:05 Jenna hooking up the IV again
5:25 Temp 37.5

Then, at 5:30, we had a discussion with Dr. G, Dr. L, and two nurses about the new results the doctors had found.

This is how my dad explained it for our family and friends in his post on the forum:

Harriet's leukemia cells are rather special and unusual. They looked visually initially like ALL cells that had "gone bad" but that was a "red herring." Certainly not ALL. The cell "malformation" or the "bad cells" seem to show some characteristics of NK cell leukemia and some characteristics of AML leukemia. "Pure" NK cell leukemia is rare. Marker CD56 is seen. Markers CD4 and CD20 are also involved somehow. Johns Hopkins University was involved in figuring this out, or helping to, in the USA. Because of the somewhat special and less common nature of Harriet's case, the Doctors suggest that it is prudent to start thinking about HLA typing because a Bone Marrow Transplant may be the best way forward in this case. If a BMT is required, it is not a big deal, surgically, anymore. Stem cells are harvested from a donor who simply gives blood (anywhere in the world), then Harriet receives the BMT through the IV! (No surgery.)

He used an exclamation mark. He used the word *special* twice. He literally said *not a big deal*, as if to try and reassure us, especially himself, that everything was fine.

What I remember of this meeting: sitting in between my parents on a peach-coloured sofa in the "family room," perhaps chosen since it was a more neutral space than my bedroom, or perhaps because the seating arrangements were more conducive to conversation. I could sit up, be involved, rather than lie prostrate in the cot. The two doctors and Jenna, my principal nurse, sat on the sofa opposite. The light was lower than in the hallways and bedrooms; yellow tones, not white. I rested my head on the shoulder of one of my parents, I can't remember which. I was tired. I don't remember hearing any more words, or saying any words, either.

The tone of the meeting was polite. Delicate. Jenna looked like she was trying not to be nervous. The doctors spoke slowly, careful with their words. I didn't look at my parents on either side of me, but I felt their presence like you feel your bed when you're more tired than you've ever been: grateful, but you always knew it was there. I felt profound exhaustion. The feeling was a collapse that was kind of like resignation, but not about recognizing the futility of trying. Rather, it was a further, deeper, submission to the system. I let go. I would let the doctors do the work of fighting the death inside of me, and I would continue to try to do the work of living.

Later that night, my mother's hand, more matter-of-fact than she usually was in the journal:

9:05pm, vitals 37.0, BP 100/60.
TPN feed back on for 17 hours.
Ate ½ bagel & cream cheese + nectarine + half peach.
Gilmore Girls then I read to her.
Ativan at 10:30pm.

oo

Cal said one of his intentions for the road trip was to learn how to be comfortable in the openness of time. "Doing nothing doesn't have to mean you're bored. Doing nothing should feel the same as doing everything. It's learning how to be comfortable in just being."

When I found out I was pregnant I thought about that, "just being," a lot; the little baby growing—and just being—inside of me. And even if I wasn't actively doing anything, I was growing a life. Making lungs, accommodating new bones, building a heart. Pregnancy is a lesson in letting go: bodies know what they are doing, just as flowers know how to bloom.

"Is there a but?" I asked Cal at one point. "Do I also have to be . . . happy?"

"No," he said, "You don't even have to be happy. You can just be."

∞

I recently found a Post-It I wrote years ago: "What if I don't want to write anything anymore? How do I just make people feel feelings?"

o

I didn't think about what any of this would have been like for my parents as individuals. *I* was the one experiencing this; *I* was the one who was sick. They were my parents, but this was about me, not them. It's revelatory and humbling to go back through these journals now and see how my illness was also something that they were experiencing, and how they were processing it, each in their own ways. The things they were seeing, the things they had to suddenly pay attention to. The fact that they hardly spent any time just the two of them for months. How they completely, instantaneously surrendered their lives in order to prioritize mine.

My mother has a university degree in home economics, and she most often made notes about what she was feeding me. Food was her medicine. Her entries are usually slightly more narrative, including conversations with the family and friends who visited; when the updates veer towards the banal, I can sense her concern between the lines.

My father, an aeronautical engineer and flying instructor, is very practiced in keeping logbooks for his work, and it's his logic and organizational system that anchor the journals. His humour comes through (there's a whole section where he annotates the loss, and then the discovery, of Lilac, my teddy bear, and how he'd asked a nurse to make a hospital-wide Code Yellow announcement); so does his hope (*special! no big deal!*). He's most often the one who transcribes the medical information and meetings with doctors.

I found a small boxed-off section at the back of the notebook in my dad's hand, no date:

MEETING WITH DR. B.
Teenager—autonomy, dependency
Sense of loss re. friends
Hormones, leave for now?
Parents as victims.
Redirect art therapy role plays control.

Parents as victims? What does this mean? That the teenager sees the parents as victims, or the parents see themselves that way? Or is it something else? The reference to hormones was regarding my ability to have children later on in life. This was the start of a conversation with the gynecological department about whether or not that would be possible, and if there was any action my parents could take now to save my fertility for later. They did, as suggested in that note, decide to leave the subject for the moment.

Technology does not exist now but could freeze, as it might in the near future.

Chemotherapy can decrease fertility, but with a bone marrow transplant I would definitely be unable to naturally conceive a child. I was a child then, though; I wasn't able to think about my own future children.

OO

The first ultrasound of our baby happens at fifteen weeks.
My hippie doctor had recommended that I wait, and only
get a scan if complications arose—"you don't know what
those sound waves do to a tiny, forming body"—but he still
gave me a prescription for one when I asked. I wanted to
see. I needed to see that it was real.

I'd had hundreds of scans of my insides before this, and it
always felt profane. There's something sacred about the body
and its mysteries, and seeing myself—heart, liver, lungs,
brain—reduced to pulp and membranes repulsed me. It
made me feel like a machine made of flesh.

For this ultrasound, I bring Cal, who isn't allowed in
the room with me until the end of the process. I'm not even
allowed to see the screen until he enters the room, too. It
must be that the technician doesn't want to deal with the
questions—"What's that? And that? Is that thing normal?"—
but also that they need to make sure everything is okay before
opening things up for dialogue.

Both of us see the black-and-white screen at the same time.

"It's a baby!" Cal says, and I know what he means. This early, neither of us was expecting to see a head and limbs in a baby shape. All I could picture was a jumble of body parts floating, disembodied.

As a precaution, before I travel overseas, my doctor gives me the ultrasound examination report. Obviously, I open the envelope.

Spine: unremarkable.

Brain: unremarkable.

Heart: unremarkable.

But my baby, I think, indignant, is *completely* remarkable!

Shortly after the ultrasound, I have to have a series of standard blood tests and other minor procedures to make sure the baby is developing correctly. Like when I brought the kids I was babysitting to the blood test that foreshadowed my disease, I now have someone for whom I need to brave my fear of needles. In this process, I begin to learn, in an embodied way, something I had known intellectually but never yet fully felt—that I'm no longer the child, no longer the subject.

○

The first time anyone in my family heard the term "Natural Killer," it was from the mouth of one of the first doctors who'd seen me in Emergency. This doctor was a middle-aged man who wore white button-up shirts over his large belly and tucked them in to khakis, a large pager hanging off his belt buckle. He was kind, had a loud laugh. One month in, my parents saw him in the hallway and he stopped to chat and ask how I was doing.

My dad told him that the "CD56 tag had been identified."

"Oh, really?" the doctor said. "So it's the Natural Killer?"

I pictured my mum crumpling into my dad's arms, but I learned, years later, that it was actually my dad who crumpled. By the glass windows looking over the atrium, up on the eighth floor.

It's a long way to fall.

○

Natural Killer cells are a type of white blood cell in everyone's bodies; they're an integral part of the immune systems of many animals. They were only discovered recently; their behaviours were noted for the first time in the 1970s, and even at the time of my diagnosis, the technology to properly identify these cells was developing concurrently with my treatment.

Unlike other white blood cells, Natural Killers don't follow orders in any kind of chain of command: they are autonomous, and can identify and kill targets on their own. The cells are so good at their jobs that they can even trigger other cells to kill *themselves*.

Among Natural Killers' main targets are the cells in our bodies that mutate and become cancerous. This happens fairly regularly in all healthy people: a cell makes a mistake, chooses the wrong path, and Natural Killer cells find them and kill them before they propagate. They are able to do this because they can distinguish self from non-self, and even self from "altered self": they can recognize the self that has turned against itself. They often misidentify the first, newly growing cells of an embryo to be a foreign body attacking their host, and as a result, Natural Killers are responsible for many miscarriages.

In my case, the Natural Killers had become cancerous. The cancer fighters were themselves malignant. The soldiers had betrayed the army; my cells were turncoats.

My medical team at Sick Kids partnered with hematology and oncology specialists around the world in order to help research my particular cancer, which, as my dad had noted in the meeting with the doctors, was "somewhat special and less common." Doctors at Johns Hopkins Hospital in Baltimore were involved, as well as specialists at institutions in Japan and England. All of the doctors weighed in to determine my treatment protocol, and at the beginning, all of them recommended the bone marrow transplant.

I invested all of my faith and trust in my doctors, and in medicine in general. I surrendered my body to them. Now I can see this was a survival mechanism. It was only when I came to hear phrases like "the specialists are debating" or "there isn't a consensus among the team" that I was even slightly aware that there wasn't a sure, straight, and clear path I had to walk down in order to reach my future healthy self. The doctors were figuring it out as they went. I was blazing a trail.

Only six people had previously been diagnosed with Natural Killer leukemia, and none of them had survived.

Now, I type "Natural Killer Leukemia" into Google:

- An article published in 2009, seven years after my diagnosis: "On review of the English-language literature only 68 published cases were identified"
- Aggressive chemotherapy followed by a stem cell transplant "appears to slightly prolong overall survival, but relapse is almost inevitable"
- From *Nature* magazine: Natural Killer leukemia is "catastrophic"
- It is "the rarest and worst malignancy"
- Median survival time of Natural Killer leukemia is 58 days
- There are "no known survivors"
- "The clinical progression is inexorable despite treatment"

Inexorable. Relentless, inescapable. I hadn't known.

I keep searching the Internet, wanting to find evidence of myself as the exception. "No known survivors except, in 2002, a fifteen-year-old female from Toronto." I can't find this *except,* though.

I need people to know that I exist, that their experiment worked, that by some combination of luck and science, I'm alive.

∞

People always ask me whether I was scared. Whether I thought I was going to die. Part of the answer is that I don't think that I ever truly understood the scope of what was happening to me. I'm not sure whether fully comprehending this would be possible for anyone, let alone a child. And not knowing can be helpful. In many ways, I chose not to look at things directly.

When they identified the involvement of the Natural Killer cells, I asked one of the young resident doctors what my odds of survival were. I remember him sitting across from my hospital cot, his legs crossed. "Well," he said, "since nobody else has survived it, and it's combined with something else, we just don't know." Somehow, this did not daunt me. *They don't know!* I thought. *So it could be good!*

Another part of the answer is that I just didn't accept death as a possibility. I'm not saying I "chose to survive," or that it had anything to do with bravery. It was a combination of luck and circumstance, nothing else. Saying survival is about anything else—bravery, or love, or optimism, or faith of any kind—would mean that those who do not survive are lacking those things. Like, someone died because they weren't *brave*? Bullshit.

(Survival itself seems too loaded a word. *Survivor* is a reality show, a feminist anthem, a syndrome caused by guilt. I'd rather just say, I lived.)

I guess what I'm trying to say is that a gun was held to my head and I couldn't look down the black hole of its barrel, or feel the cold metal on my skin. I had to look straight ahead and keep on walking.

oo

When I first saw the van it was an evening in November and my stomach sank as we sat in the cold, dark, tiny box, but I tried to be enthusiastic. It's no longer than an average car, and I couldn't imagine folding my life up that small for a whole summer. I didn't go back inside until the spring, a bright, warm morning. The van was parked on the street and Cal popped the top, zipped open the three windows in the canvas, and I lay like a happy cat in the sun.

We set off four weeks later.

Let me give you a little tour: there's a bench in the back that folds down to become a bed (this is where the dogs sleep) and folds up if you find yourself parked in front of the ocean and want to sit and enjoy the view. There's a canvas tent-like extension that pops open so you can stand upright for about four square feet—this is convenient for cooking, as it's right above the "kitchen." When the top is popped, another bed-frame extends—Cal insists on calling it "the second bedroom"—and this is where we sleep.

There are now five heartbeats in the tiny space, but at least we have the whole world for our living room.

○

Nothing was mine. It wasn't my bed, my door, my table. It was the hospital's bed, the hospital's door, the hospital's table, and I was just occupying the space. It started feeling like not even my body was my body—my body had turned against me.

At some point, either my dad or I started calling the IV pump "Ivy." "The nurse has to change Ivy's tubes," we'd say, or "Will Ivy fit in there with you?" It didn't feel anthropomorphic or cute; it felt accurate. This machine connected to me felt like part machine and part pet; part self and part other. A symbiotic thing, not quite alive, but not entirely unalive, either.

The nurses performed a careful choreography to time the drugs and blood transfusions. Chemo couldn't hang at the same time as a transfusion or the drugs would eradicate the fresh blood; certain drugs needed a bolus of liquid to be injected quickly before administering them; antibiotics needed to be meted out between chemotherapy doses. If there was ever a moment when there was no bag of drugs or blood or liquid food hanging, saline was hung at a steady drip in order to "keep the lines open." The lines of my veins, or the lines of the machine, or both. They were essentially the same thing.

Because of the fever and the infection I'd contracted, I had to continue straight through to the second round without going home in between, as we'd hoped. I say we, but at that point, I don't think I was hoping for anything like that: I could only focus on what was in front of me. I had already accepted that I'd be in the hospital for six months. After that, I said to myself, like a prayer or a promise, I'd be cured.

○

Nurses performed dressing changes every couple of days. A friend was in my room when a nurse came to say she had to change my dressing, and I had to explain it wasn't about my clothes, and I didn't mind if she stayed in the room while it happened.

The point on my chest where the tubing entered my skin was susceptible to infection, as it was basically a constant open wound. It was covered with a thin, clear plastic sheet, about the size of a playing card, which stuck right onto my skin, and on top of that was gauze and porous tape. This covering system had to be changed every couple of days; more often if it got especially wet, or started getting itchy or red.

My aunt was swapping in for my parents during a dressing change, and she noted in the book: *I asked Harriet if this bothered her. She said "No."*

But thinking about it now makes me so uncomfortable that I can't believe I would have said it didn't bother me.

I can hardly write about it. Putting my mind into that memory, I want to recoil.

The raw patch of puckered skin touching air was so tender it felt painful, but more than that, I'd become so terrified of germs that having this flesh, which I'd been told was so sensitive, exposed—

It made breathing difficult.

Once the tape and sticky sheet had been removed, like ripping off a Band-Aid, the nurse had to wipe it all down with a Q-tip covered in rubbing alcohol or hydrogen peroxide (whichever it was, it was something that stung). They'd have to let it dry for a few moments—during which time nobody, not the nurse, not me, not anyone else in the room, was allowed to breathe near me at risk of transferring germs. I held my breath. I let it go, looking at the ceiling. Once it was dry, they put a new dressing on.

The scar is the size of a nickel now, still shiny and pink. I couldn't touch it then, and can't even now. It falls about two inches below my right collarbone. You can see it when I wear a tank top or bathing suit. When people notice it, they don't usually comment on it—it's that kind of serious-looking.

∞

Writing this, I have to look at myself in a way that I never did then: as a victim. (*Victim*: target, prey, object.) Writing about myself as a subject, I must subject myself to a sort of narrative.

O

Having no control over my life in any micro- or macroscopic way, I became very assertive in whatever way I could. I would demand spaghetti or steak or strawberries, and expect the craving to be instantly fulfilled. For the most part, it was. There was one particular nurse whose demeanour I found patronizing, and I told the head nurse that I no longer wanted her attending to me. I never saw her again.

There was also one particular doctor whom I liked the best: he had a smooth South African accent and a haircut like my dad's. Once when I was scared I asked to see him, and only him. I'd felt a bump in my arm and was sure it was a tumour. That my cancer was spreading, becoming something solid.

When he didn't respond to his pager, an announcement went out over the entire hospital PA system requesting that this doctor please come to my room as soon as possible. After twenty minutes or so—he might have been in surgery or something, I have no idea—he came to my room, quickly but not rushing. He listened to me, felt around the lump with a thorough tenderness, and after careful reflection he said the bump was not a tumour, it was just a belated reaction of a vein to of one of the peripheral ivs I'd had. The vein was temporarily clogged. This wasn't a symptom of my dying, he promised me, at least not in the way that I'd feared.

My underlying question for him was: What next? If I leave here, will I live? If I leave here, how long for? If I leave, will I ever be truly well again?

Just like being able to accept that I would stay in the hospital for six months and then be cured, I was also able to accept that I would always be vulnerable to sickness. These two truths didn't contradict one another in my mind: they were two sides of the same coin. I believed that, after the cancer had been eradicated, I would need regular, perhaps aggressive maintenance. I never wanted to leave my body unwatched. I expected I'd always have to sleep with one eye open.

"How do you imagine it going?" the doctor asked me. "If you were going to be always on alert, what would that look like?"

"I'd come and get blood tests and full-body CT scans every week to make sure there were no cancer cells developing," I said. "For the rest of my life."

He nodded. "That kind of thing wouldn't be necessary," he said.

At the time I took this as a good sign—a sign of hope—but I realize now that it was, in fact, completely neutral. Not a promise at all.

OO

The road trip starts on a Friday in May, and on Monday, we have our first minor disaster. That day, we stop for lunch and a walk in Grand Falls, a stunning natural gorge in New Brunswick. The churning, eternal chaos of the waterfall reminds me of the power and mystery of the natural world.

We plan on setting up camp for the night on Crown land in northern New Brunswick. Shortly after leaving Grand Falls, though, on the highway towards the forest, we lose cellphone reception. It doesn't come back.

"Does that make you nervous?" I ask.

"No," Cal says, "why would it?"

We approach the unnamed, unpaved road he's flagged as a potential camp spot, but it's steep, covered in snow, and leads to a visible dead end.

"Let's try the next one," I suggest.

The next one doesn't look much better, but it has less snow and less of an incline, and Cal thinks the van can handle it. It can't, and we spend the next two hours trying to fill the wet ditches with snow, wedging sticks underneath the tires and pushing the van while reversing it. All this shifts us by about a foot, not nearly enough.

Night is falling, and we are stuck in mud in a snowy forest off an unnamed road with no cell reception, a hundred kilometres from the nearest town. For the second time that day, I am reminded of the power and mystery of the natural world.

The isolation makes me nervous. The dogs are wet and filthy from the swampy ground, the damp, dark forest makes the van unbearably cold, and I won't be able to hop out of the van in the night to pee, as I need to do every few hours. In this moment, we can't "just be"; we have to "just do." We need to get out of there. At this moment, it feels to me as though the van—this literal and symbolic home—has let us down. My grief is perhaps weighted more towards the symbolic than the literal, but my sense of urgency is compounded by fear and wanting to protect our unborn baby.

I tell Cal to walk back to the highway and flag someone down to help us, and the first person who drives by stops immediately. While François, a former tow truck driver, doesn't think he can help us get the van unstuck, he is willing to give us a ride.

"All of us? Including the dogs?"

All four of us hitch a ride to Miramichi, the nearest town, which is ninety minutes away. In Miramichi, I say to myself, we will be able to get reception and call for a tow truck. We will be able to eat and sleep and be warm again.

François drops us off at a hotel in the industrial outskirts of the city. There is a huge NO PETS sign at the entrance, but seeing us walk into the lobby at eleven p.m. with no vehicle in the parking lot, the receptionist reads the desperation crumpling our bodies and books us into a room at the far end of a quiet hallway.

Once we get into our room, Cal calls CAA and, within minutes, a tow truck is there to drive him back to the middle of the mint-gum green hexagon where we'd landed on the Google Map. I stay with the dogs and order pizza from the only place in town that isn't closed.

Lying in the hotel bed, the exhausted dogs wrestling each other to sleep, I text a friend. I am still deep in lingering anxiety, but also a kind of shame at having wound up here, in what feels like a worst-case scenario. I have the fear I sometimes get about there only being one right way for me to live, and that we've made the wrong move.

She responds:

How can you be upset? You're in the perfect situation!
A warm bed with pizza! And this is what you signed up for!
This is an adventure!

∞

If it's information I'm legally supposed to tell my dentist then
it feels like an omission to not tell new friends, first dates:
a warning, almost. This is part of my weather system, written
into my personal constellations, something I think about both
all the time and not at all. A baseline. A starting point.

I moved away from home when I was eighteen, just two
years after my treatment ended. I studied at a university
a thirty-hour drive from where I'd grown up. Though
I didn't consider this at the time, looking back I can now see
I was wanting to experience as many things as possible. I was
hungry, thirsty, insatiable, and the danger of relapse was like
my shadow, at my heels. I was also running from a world
where everyone knew I had been sick, which is ironic,
I know, when all I wanted to do was tell all the new people
I met about how I had been sick.

When I met my first friend in Halifax, I told her abruptly
as we walked up the stairs to my dorm room. She had

dreadlocks, was a year older than me, and was married to a man she'd met at Christian boarding school. I told her as we walked, her a few steps behind me, so we weren't facing each other. I just wanted her to know, and then we could move on.

Going away to university I felt so adult, and that my experience with illness was long behind me. And yet: in my student ID photo from first year, my hair is still short, growing out at different lengths. It would be another several years before I would be considered out of the risk of relapse.

As we read ancient philosophical and religious texts, my friend and I learned to doubt together. We learned to ask questions to which we'd never thought we were missing the answers.

Now, thirteen years later, she no longer has dreadlocks, is married to a new man, and we are pregnant at the same time. She's already had two children, one of whom died at birth. This tragedy marked, for her, a new phase in doubting. We are now both afraid of our bodies' potential to betray.

○

I'm not sure who told the first person, or the pattern of how the message spread, but, thankfully, at the time of my diagnosis, I never had to tell anyone. Suddenly, everyone just knew.

All of my close friends each have their own story of hearing of my diagnosis. They remember it as a bad event that happened to them.

My friend from next door's story is that her mom picked her up from school and had *A Walk to Remember* sitting on the passenger seat as a present. The movie had just come out on VHS and would be something bonding for them to do together that evening after discussing my diagnosis. Her mother told her on the drive home, they both cried, she asked questions for which there weren't yet answers, and then they sat together on the couch to watch Mandy Moore. The back of the box only revealed that "a heart-breaking secret" would put the couple's relationship to the test and they'd realize "the true meaning of love and fate." Her mom had no idea that the movie was about leukemia when she chose it.

Jamie, played by Mandy Moore, is a young, beautiful woman who withers at the apex of her youth and beauty. Jamie finally confesses to her boyfriend Landon that she's not applying to college for the fall, or hoping to join the Peace Corps. Confused, he asks what she's going to do.

"I'm sick," she says, turning to face him.

Landon, practical in his ignorance, isn't worried: he says he'll just take her home, then.

Jamie, suddenly incredibly frustrated that he doesn't understand that when she said *sick* she meant *dying*, cries, "No! Landon! I'm sick." Her eyes fill with tears. "I have leukemia."

Landon, understandably, is surprised. "No," he says, laughing, unable to reconcile the image of his beautiful, long-haired girlfriend, with whom he's just been striding arm in arm down the sidewalk, with the image we all have in our heads of a person with leukemia. Landon can't believe it. "You're eighteen," he says. "You're perfect."

What if sickness and perfection have nothing to do with one another?

Years later, my friend laughed telling me this. "Can you believe that? Of all the movies she picked, it was one about a teenager getting leukemia. It's like, too good to be true."

June 24, 2:30 p.m.

Hello everyone. Good news. Dr. A reported that the first round of chemo was very successful, the leukemia HAS BEEN DRIVEN INTO REMISSION. Remission is defined as <5%, and Harriet has much less than 5%, driven down from more than 90%. Round 2 should start as soon as possible. Dr. A also signed wig form.

June 25, 6:05 a.m.

The second round of Chemo started last night as expected, so 24 June was "Day 1" of round 2. It's 5 days of Chemo then recovery with a target of a new bone marrow aspirate & lumbar puncture on Day 21. It is much more comfortable for Harriet now that the Central IV Line is installed in her chest, rather than an IV line in the arm, which she had for the first few days of the first round. There are IV Chemo meds & tablet Chemo meds. The second dose in the IV was at about 4am this morning (I did not wake up properly, Harriet did not call for me, and even Harriet essentially slept through it) ☺

We're all trying to learn and do things better than the first round, so Harriet is getting up & about more, keeping mobile & spending time standing or sitting (too much lying down is not good for the lungs etc), and we have to try harder this time to protect her from catching any "bugs," especially when her white counts are low.

That's all for now. Things are going well.

David

∞

I've been told—of the novel version of this book, as well as this non-fiction version—that I should describe the narrator before she got sick. That people should get a sense of who I was before all this. But the thing is, I was the same person before I got sick. I don't believe in the transformative power of illness, either for good or for bad.

oo

My parents are now of grandparent age. When we tell them we're expecting a baby, my mum uses the word "miracle." A word I find a little embarrassing, too ostentatious. I don't believe this event to be divine, even if it is, in accordance with the definition of that word, unexpected according to the laws of nature and science.

("Well," my gynecologist said, "clearly the chemo didn't affect your fertility, then!")

My parents live in a bungalow overlooking a pond near Georgian Bay, and my mum, looking out at the frozen water, says she can't wait to see the baby one day paddling in the shallows. She'll have to get a little toy fishing rod, she says.

But the baby is just the size of a Barbie doll, I think, still living inside of me. An unborn Barbie doll couldn't possibly go fishing.

This feeling is apparently common among expecting mothers, the feeling that the baby doesn't exist beyond its current state, whether that's when it's the size of a pea, or a lemon, or a cantaloupe, or when it's a three-month old baby. Some call it being superstitious, but I think it's being reasonable. Studies show that fathers, and everyone else, don't have this problem of imagining the future. I wonder what this comes down to.

Our mothers are our first home, and they are the first thing we leave behind when we enter the world. I think my mum found it harder to stand back and see my illness as being about me, and not as an experience that was happening to her, to her daughter. But, as my family doctor said about my pregnancy, it was about us both. I was the one with cancer, but she was the one whose child was sick.

From a very young age, I had the sense that I made my mother afraid, that she felt she had created something that was beyond her, something that she couldn't control or comprehend. Fear can be a form of love, I think, and this love-fear I perceived intensified when I got cancer. Her love was so big and her fear was infinite. My genes—my cells, my chromosomes—had mutated and grown far beyond her, and she did not have the power to make me well. Had my mother, I wonder, felt responsible for my illness? Had she felt as though the seed of my death had grown within her?

A mother's love is, to me, a given (I realize this speaks of my good fortune); but a child's love for their mother is not. This asymmetry is newly painful to me. A child can never—maybe even from an evolutionary perspective, *should* never—love their parents as much as their parents love them.

While I am pregnant, love and fear are constant, merging, opposing, unifying forces. What if I don't love my child. What if my child doesn't love me. What if we both love each other more than we can imagine and then one of us—me, hopefully—dies, and the love becomes uprooted, nowhere to grow. What happens to our love when we die?

○

Midway through my treatment, one of my doctors came into my room when neither of my parents was there and told me, out of the blue: "In my religion, people get sick with illnesses like yours as punishments for crimes they've committed in past lives."

This is another way of phrasing "everything happens for a reason." In his case, the reason was very specific, though the specifics were unknown.

Where does that expression come from, *out of the blue*? Is this where the cancer had come from? That big, infinite blue? Blue means sky, blue means sadness. Both of those are infinite, I suppose.

There's no logic to childhood cancers the way there is with certain adult cancers. A seventy-year-old who's been smoking for the last fifty-five years might learn of their lung cancer diagnosis with a certain regret, but the risk was known and they chose to take it.

In this case, being born was the risk.

In the belief system presented to me by this doctor, the risk originated long before that. Who did he think was to blame? Who was my past self, and what had she done to deserve this?

∞

I was baptized as a baby and went to church regularly. Three of my aunts and uncles are priests. I taught Sunday school and went to Christian camp for a couple of summers (my best friend was going and I wanted to do whatever she did). But I've never really felt religious. I've felt awe and a sense of mystery, and an obligation to be reverent to that awe.

Religious or not, it's commonplace to talk about God in a hospital. "Everything happens for a reason," one of the phrases I heard most often, is deeply entrenched in an understanding of a higher power, and the underlying belief that there is a preordained order choreographing our lives and our deaths.

What is the reason for my getting sick?

What is the reason that so many kids die?

That first summer at Christian camp I would have been eleven or twelve, and our camp counsellors were sixteen or so. Every day there was Bible study, hymn singing, prayers, and evening vespers, where the kids in each cabin would sit around discussing particular themes with their counsellors. Our counsellor was named Batman—we were never told their real names. Batman was skinny and freckly with a piggish nose and Miss Piggy curls.

I don't remember what the subject of conversation was that night, but I was prompted to ask: "What if you don't believe that God makes the sun rise every morning, or makes each flower bloom, or makes the tides come and go, but that he made the world so that it could do those things on its own?"

There was a moment of silence as Batman thought about this, and then she said: "Well, then you're going to hell."

I didn't listen to anything for the rest of the night. Feeling bullied into belief, I tried to pray to an image of a God I didn't think existed so as to, as the counsellors said, "let Jesus into my heart."

Deep into the night, I whispered to my best friend, two bunk beds over, also on top.

"Are you awake?"

"Yes."

"Can I come over?"

"Please," she said.

I scurried down my ladder, up hers, and we held each other, our tiny bodies in that tiny twin bed, finding faith not in God but in friendship.

○

My dad never frowned: he raised his eyebrows instead. As a result, he always looked surprised when he was in thought, rather than stern or heavily pensive. I once asked why he did this, and he said it was so that his face wouldn't look mean when he got old and wrinkled. He was training it to stay as kind as he was.

He was on duty for Father's Day. That's how my parents phrased it: being "on duty," like a job, like a war. It was after dinner, a twilight sky outside of my sterile room, and I suddenly felt overwhelmed with guilt that, because of me, my parents had to spend so much of their time in a hospital.

I told him I was sorry I was sick, that we had to be in the hospital for this day, that I hadn't done anything special for him, that he had to spend so much time here in general. He had his back to me. His body started to tremble, like wind shaking the trees before a storm. He shook his head, then turned to look at me. He was crying. Not just teary-eyed, but weeping.

"No, Harriet," he said, "No. You have nothing to be sorry about."

That was the only time I'd ever seen him cry.

○

I'd been lying down in bed for so long that most of the nurses and doctors had never seen me standing up. By fifteen I was already at my full height, which was much taller than the younger kids on the ward, and I still had enough of my own hair to look normal; many of the medical staff didn't recognize me when they saw me standing, pushing my IV along the hallway. When I told them my name, their faces changed. I looked so much less sick than my diagnosis would have had them expect.

MONDAY JULY 1 *(written in my own hand)*:
12:10pm Going for a walk w my leg weights and dad

Though I wrote only ten words, that unpunctuated sentence opens up a whole memory to inhabit that would likely otherwise be lost. I went to the main elevators in the hallway; there were three on either side, forming the central spine of the hospital's architecture, each with glass windows that offered a view of the atrium as you slid up and down, smooth as music. Next to each elevator was a flight of stairs. I couldn't stray far from the tethered length of my IV, and distance wasn't the point—I just had to use the muscles that were beginning to atrophy. My dad strapped blue Velcro weights to my ankles and I went down three steps until the IV tubes were pulled taut, then back up. I did this three or four times—nine or twelve steps in total—before becoming too tired to continue. We walked back to the room, and I stayed in bed for the rest of the day.

o

A two-year-old called Megan was admitted to the room opposite mine. When she came to the emergency ward it was because her eyes were swollen with what turned out to be growths burgeoning behind her eyeballs, her dad told me. Cancer had been growing in her body for nearly half of her life: she was diagnosed with AML before her second birthday. We were given many of the same drugs, and because she was too young to vocalize her experience, I sometimes went over to tell her parents, who were both pretty young themselves, about certain side effects I was having. One of the drugs hurt to go in, another made my mouth taste funny. I thought it might be helpful for them to hear what it felt like from someone other than a pharmacist, from someone first-hand.

One day when I was over in her room across the hall from mine, her dad said to me something that he'd clearly prepared: "Megan seems so much happier now than she was before coming to the hospital. She was always grumpy before—I think now she's more grateful for life."

I nodded, not knowing what else to do, not thinking of the fact that he was talking about his two-year-old child, a little baby girl who'd been incredibly, inexplicably ill for much of her life.

"I bet it's the same for you, right, Harriet? You're probably a lot happier and more grateful for life now that you're in here, right?"

Again, I just nodded. Megan's father was twenty-three years old and had had two children by the time he was twenty; but being only fifteen years old myself, he seemed to me like someone with authority whose word I should trust.

I went back to my room, feeling unsettled. What he'd said wasn't mean, or even really all that negative. It made me uncomfortable, though, with its echoes of "everything happens for a reason." It mirrored, too, what the doctor had told me about his religious system. What this man had said was connected to a system of cause and effect, of crime and punishment.

I didn't tell anyone what he'd said to me, but the next day, a nurse I really liked—a young woman who was probably also only twenty-three or so—came to my room nearly in tears.

"Harriet?" She wasn't my nurse that evening, but I could tell she was there for a reason. She was wearing a bright pink t-shirt and dark blue Modrobes and had a low ponytail and pink cheeks. Her voice was high-pitched and unsure of itself, but she pushed through it: "Megan's dad told me what he said to you yesterday, and he seemed really proud of himself, like he'd just taught you this important lesson, but I really needed to tell you that he's wrong. He doesn't know what he's talking about, it doesn't make any sense. You are such a lovely, strong, happy young woman, and I'm sure you were like that even before you were sick. You didn't get sick for any reason, and you don't have to be more grateful for anything now. I wish he hadn't said that to you. I wanted to make sure you're okay."

I started to cry. The nurse hugged me.

∞

Difficult experiences are often used as "material" later;
this is often even given as consolation during the experience.
At least you'll get some good stories out of this! At fifteen,
I wasn't thinking of being a writer. Did the "material" make
me a writer? Is this ascribing a transformative effect to
illness, which I said I didn't believe in?

○

During the second round of chemo, one of my nurses took my dad and me through a back hallway to visit the bone marrow transplant ward. The transplant the doctors had mentioned in that diagnostic meeting was scheduled to happen after four rounds of chemo, after I had recovered my immune system and once a match had been found.

It's impossible to determine how long it takes for a match to be found, so nobody would give me a date for when the transplant would take place. I thought it would happen instantaneously, and was disappointed when I found out it was rather indefinitely on hold. The search process takes a long time. There was nothing to do but wait, and I was so sick of waiting.

Both of my parents, and each of their parents, as well as *their* parents, are from England. This means that, even though I don't have siblings who would share my DNA, it can be easier to find a higher-level genetic match for the ten blood factors. The goal was a 10/10 match, but anything over a 7/10 was acceptable.

There was a three-year-old boy on the ward at the same time as me whose mother was Haitian and whose father was Egyptian. The doctors were looking for a bone marrow match for him but couldn't find one. The little boy died of meningitis he'd contracted from his own body.

The nurse wanted to show me what the BMT ward was like so I could prepare myself for when the time came. Even before going, I knew it was going to be different. Hard.

Each room in the unit is airlocked, with two sealing doors. The patient remains in the room, within both doors, at all times. Only three registered guests are ever allowed to go inside the room—parents, a sibling, a friend. Three in total.

The way that the BMT was presented to me made it seem like my only hope at salvation.

Because of the somewhat special and less common nature of Harriet's case . . .

So even though seeing the rooms stunned me, I had been able to convince my brain to not be afraid of the process but to look *forward* to it. If it was my chance at being cured, then it didn't make sense to be afraid.

I tried to remember this even as I learned that I would not be able to eat food that wasn't boiled or canned for up to a year after the BMT. That I would have to take steroids to prevent the very likely event that my body rejected the transplant. That my eggs and ovaries, if they happened to still be fertile after all the chemotherapy, would certainly have any life finally burned out of them by the preparation for the transplant, unless an ovary was removed ahead of time and frozen in the hopes that, as my dad had noted, *technology might exist later*. That I would inherit the allergies and DNA of my donor: meaning, if I received stem cells from a man, my blood would register as male. (The different DNA part was actually cool, I thought. My first thought was that I'd be able to commit crimes and not get caught.)

The nurse, my dad, and I stood looking around this airlocked room. In between the two sets of doors was a sterilization station, where nurses, doctors, and the registered guests would have to completely wash and sterilize their hands, arms, and faces, and then gear up in full-body suits. Gloves, booties that went over the shoes, a mask to cover the mouth and nose, and a cap to cover the head. For months, I would see only eyes.

"Well," my dad said, not looking at either the nurse or me. "This is good to see, isn't it?"

It was like being in the middle of a hailstorm in the summer and saying, "Lovely weather we're having for the time of year!"

oo

People ask if I can feel the baby yet. It'll feel like flutters, they say.

How am I supposed to know what to feel? I want to ask them. My body is constantly giving me feelings I don't understand.

But when I do start feeling the baby move, and the wriggles are significant enough for Cal to be able to sense with his palms to my belly, I finally feel as though this isn't all in my head. The little surprised half-smile of delight I see from Cal when he can feel a tiny flutter from deep within my body brings me, even weeks later, such joy.

The first stranger to comment on my baby-belly is a fishmonger in Chéticamp, in the Cape Breton highlands, who sells us freshly caught trout that we carry from his van to ours.

"Really?" I want to hug him. "You see this too?"

That night, as we fry up the fish for dinner, I ask Cal, "What are you most afraid of?"

"In life?" he asks.

"No," I say, "About the baby." I had thought this was implicit.

Though it is early June, our more northern, coastal position means that the temperature drops below zero as soon as the sun falls. As I cook, the sun low in the sky, Cal starts to build a fire to prepare against the coming cold. The dogs are lying on the ground outside, wanting to be equally close to both of us.

"Oh. I don't really have any fears."

"What? None?"

"Well," he says, lighting the fire, "we haven't been given any reason to worry about anything, and there's no point worrying for nothing. That's too abstract."

I want to laugh. Abstraction has never stopped me.

But at the same time, we both agree now that neither of us pictured the baby—what it looked like, what it would be like to hold—before it was born. Superstitious or not, we agreed that it did feel too abstract.

I slice tomatoes and fresh bread, toss them into the pan to warm through, and we eat in the last of the daylight. In the brief moments after the sun is gone behind the green hills but before the light has completely disappeared, the delicate white flowers all around us glow like tiny stars.

○

Between the second and third round of chemo, I was able to
go home. Leaving the hospital, I saw the world as if I'd just
put on glasses. Everything sharper, magnified. I saw leaves,
not trees. Feathers, not birds. My face was pressed against
the back window as we drove up the smooth bends of the
Don Valley Parkway. I was going home for the first time in
six weeks, the longest I'd ever been away.

You're never able to smell what your own home smells of,
but walking in the front door after having been in a sterile
place for so long, I could get close: pancakes, lemon, fresh
air, and potpourri.

I walked around slowly—there were so many more stairs
than I was used to—and took it all in. My own *bathroom*!
My own *bedroom*! Not having Ivy following me around, not
having someone sleeping on a vinyl couch at my side, no
beeping in the night, no announcements all day, *curtains*!

July 4: It's amazing the things I always used to take for granted and not even realize . . . like being able to flush my toilet!! (at the hospital the nurses had to test and measure all my pee . . . ugh) We have a nurse that comes to the house every day to flush my IV line (which is only about 5 inches long now, with no Ivy at the end!) and put in Heparin so that it doesn't clot up, but my dad has quickly learned how to do it himself (with the nurse's approval) so now she doesn't have to come! 😄 I get to stay at home until the 15th (when I have another bone marrow aspirate and lumbar puncture to see how things are going) or until I get sick 😷 which the nurses say is what usually comes first 😕 So I've been bringing little anti-bacterial hand wipes everywhere and using them all the time and staying as far away from everybody as I can.

I did get to go to the mall yesterday 😄 which was great, especially since it wasn't very crowded.

I don't know much about the third round of chemo, but hopefully it will run as smoothly as the second one. I think that it's shorter, but stronger and more condensed but I don't know.

The self-imposed no-touching rule continued: the last thing I wanted to do was land myself back in the hospital any earlier than absolutely necessary. When I went to the mall with friends I Purelled my hands every five minutes. We had family over for dinner, and I didn't touch any of them, or any of the things they brought. These were my own rules— no doctors or nurses had advised this—but I felt so afraid, and so vulnerable, that it was one thing I could do to feel a little bit more in control.

My forum update concluded:

> It's such a beautiful day outside today, so I hope I can enjoy it while it lasts . . . I'm trying to fill myself with beautiful happy things and thoughts to last me through my next hospital stay.

Re. Harriet Lye

Conducted home visit on July 4th, 2002. Both parents and Harriet participated. No complaints of nausea, appetite reasonable. Was having trouble sleeping since discharge from 8A. Parents seem to have a good grasp of diagnosis and treatment, and the seriousness of Harriet's particular illness. Mom stated that what is most important to them is information on how to help Harriet through this and to keep her well. Mrs. Lye asked about psychologic supports for Harriet. Mom requested a psych referral which I have made.

After Harriet left the room mom shared with me concerns around future fertility, and stated that she felt this would be an important issue for Harriet. At that point this had not been raised with Harriet.

I contacted Harriet's school in June and explained diagnosis. She was made exempt from her exams because of excellent academic standing. I will contact school again in September to arrange for home tutoring. Harriet does not feel a class visit is needed.

This is a high functioning family under tremendous stress. Will continue to follow.

K. D.
RN MScN

O

One of the first things I did when out of the hospital was go to a wig shop. Money had been raised for me—wigs are very expensive—and I went with my parents to a place on the fancy part of Avenue Road to try some on. At this point I still had my hair; to an outsider, I probably still looked normal.

The people at the wig shop gave me a choice. Did I want to shave my head before my hair all fell out? Some people found the process of losing it too painful to endure, and preferred to do away with it all at once. They could do it for me right there, they said—it would only take a few minutes.

"Definitely not," I said. "What if it doesn't even end up falling out? What if it stays for a long time?"

I could tell from their expressions that everyone thought I was being foolish, but looking back at it now, my response feels like a metaphor for my optimism.

Was I optimistic, though? In looking through my medical records I found a note from one of my nurses in the daily progress reports from June 3:

Emotional support provided to family. Mum very tearful when discussing hair loss for Harriet. Mum states Harriet doesn't want to have hair cut + very anxious to have hair loss. Childlife specialist visited patient to try to discuss options— difficult to have pt open up.

Of course I was anxious, but does anxiety preclude optimism? Where I remember feeling optimistic, was I in fact simply trying to delay the inevitable?

July 16: I've been at home for exactly two weeks now! When I go back to hospital for clinic visits to check my blood all the doctors and nurses are so surprised that I've lasted so long without getting an infection, especially since I've been nutripenic (sp?) for part of the time. They are also surprised that I have so much hair left . . . when I asked in the beginning when I would lose my hair, they said it would be all gone by the end of the first round. Well, HA! It's not! And I'm going into the third round on Thursday.

The third round is only 5 days, but I'll be having chemo 24 hours a day 😔. I was supposed to start the third round yesterday, but my blood cell counts weren't high enough. I hope they will be ready for Thursday!

I'm picking up my 2 wigs on Wednesday. They're *GORGEOUS*!! My mum is bringing the camera so we can take pictures and post them on the site, so everybody can see them.

I've seen what optimism can do for you, it works miracles—I think it's probably what worked for me, because I still have lots of hair, eyelashes, eyebrows, all that stuff that I was told would be all gone by about a month ago!! I mean, they are going, but only when I'm on chemo and even then, it's not in huge massive clumps.

○

My dad got the photos of me trying on wigs developed quickly so we could upload them to the website as promised. They create a scenario entirely different from the reality. Recently, on the fifteenth anniversary of my diagnosis, I posted those photos to Facebook with the caption "15 years old, 15 years ago." Half of my life lived without cancer, half of my life lived with having had it. I'd been thinking about it a lot.

The pictures got over two hundred likes, but most of my friends and family didn't make the connection to the anniversary, or even to my illness. I'd posted two photos: the one on the left was me trying on a wig with long hair that looked almost exactly as my hair did then, and the photo on the right was with a short-hair wig. Laid out side by side and without any context, it looked like a before-and-after diptych of a haircut.

Against all odds, at the time the photos were taken, I still looked normal. I was able to notice that my hair was a bit thinner, but nobody else could. I had even put on a little bit of weight and didn't look as gaunt as I had during the first round of chemo. I'm wearing a tank top and a puka-shell necklace and my skin is luminous, my eyeliner perfect; the gauze package of my IV tubing is only slightly visible in one of the photos. If you weren't looking for it, you wouldn't notice it.

In both photos, I'm looking in the mirror, unaware of the photographer. I think I look a little nervous, or at least hesitant. The kind of look you get when making very important decisions. This teenage girl is looking at herself, looking so healthy, and you'd think she's preening, wondering if she really likes her outfit after all. But I'm really thinking: Is this me? This is really what's happening? Does this look like who I am? Who I will become? There was only one point when I allowed myself to question *if* I would get the chance to become. That moment hadn't come yet.

O

That period at home—another interlude—felt so normal it
verged on the surreal. The forgetting, and then remembering,
happened all the time. My mum made me raspberry pancakes
and I don't remember it ever raining. When I went in for my
bi-weekly appointments at the clinic, on the opposite corner
of the eighth floor to the ward, the nurses said they'd never
seen anyone stay home without a fever for so long. I was so
proud to have defied expectations.

Young Heracles invited me and my family up to his cottage
for a day. He drove me around in the boat, anchoring it in
a sunny spot in the bay. I don't remember saying anything,
I just remember the feeling of my whole body smiling.
A warmth all over. How special it was to be ordinary. He
was wearing a grey tank top and silver chain necklace, his
bleached spikes freshly gelled up. He was tall and strong and
had perfect teeth and a cheeky, chubby smile. There are so
many pictures of that day, of Heracles and I sitting together

on his dock, the sun behind us, our outlines blurred. One where his mom is braiding his sister's hair, and his aunt is holding up the arms of his two-year-old cousin to help her walk to get a pool noodle. One of me pretending to drive the boat. A series of my parents and me smiling at the camera, one where my mum was caught glancing at something near my feet—the dog, maybe.

The most uncanny picture is of Heracles and me sitting side by side on Muskoka chairs, his beautiful golden retriever at our feet and the baby cousin balanced on the arms of the chairs between us. Heracles positioned the chairs carefully so that we'd be facing the light. All four of us, even the dog, are smile-squinting at the camera. I'm laughing, my mouth open as if in speech. He has one arm on the dog's back and the other around the little girl, and I'm holding onto her tiny hand. It's the time just before the golden hour, sharp shadows and warm pools of light. We don't look fifteen. We look like young parents.

Zoom in, though, and you'll see the only evidence of the disjointed reality of that exquisitely beautiful day: the gauzed pouch of my IV tubing down the middle of my abdomen, visible as a bumpy shadow underneath my turquoise t-shirt.

○

Returning to the hospital for round three, my counts still weren't high enough to start chemo. I had to wait. There was nothing to do but "rest." I could be transfused, but only so much—and you can't transfuse white blood cells. My bone marrow aspirate was scheduled for Monday July 22 but kept getting postponed due to the low blood counts. I was impatient. I was concerned. I was like a born-again believer in the health-care system and this protocol, and if it wasn't going according to schedule, what would happen? Could the cancer catch up again?

On the day the operation was finally scheduled, I wasn't allowed to eat until it was completed, as I had to be anaesthetized. They call this NPO, which my dad told me stands for the Latin *nil per os*—nothing by mouth. Since my aspirate wasn't life or death, the procedure kept getting shifted down as higher-priority cases arose. All the while, I was still unable to eat.

In the notebook, I wrote about myself in the third person to keep continuity:

It's 3pm and Harriet is dying of hunger and can't STAND waiting anymore. She's scheduled into room 12, the group room, WHICH ABSOLUTELY SUCKS.

Dying of hunger, not of cancer. These were the kinds of things I was able to complain about. Anything more than that would get existential.

○

My mum set up a telephone prayer chain at the church my
family went to, where—if I understand correctly—at any
given moment, someone was calling someone else so they
could pray for me together over the phone, threading
a message that would always be alive, no matter what time it
was. Later, my mum told me she would go to a private room
in the hospital at around two p.m. each day she was there,
a time at which, as she'd shared with the prayer chain, she
felt she needed particular support. It gave her peace to sit
there, thinking of being thought of.

Is prayer the same thing as meditation? Prayer is thought
and meditation is about not thinking: is that the difference?
I didn't know if I believed in prayer, but I was grateful for all
of these people thinking about me.

There was a chaplain in the hospital who was the cousin
of some family friends. He looked like a tall, lonesome
cowboy from some past time, the 1970s or the 1870s. He had

long brown hair that he wore in a loose ponytail that hung
straight down his spine and he had a long, equine face.

I liked when the chaplain came to visit. I don't remember
what we talked about, but we never talked about God. He
was used to talking to kids who were as sick as I was as
though we were normal people, and not very many people
are good at that.

I was given a jade bracelet that had been blessed by
a monk in Tibet in my honour. The daughter of a cousin of
a family friend had travelled there, or something. (Ten years
later, I mailed the bracelet across the world again to another
girl who was dying—and then died—of cancer.)

One of my cousins travelled around Southeast Asia,
lighting candles for me in all of the temples and sacred
spaces he visited.

My Girl Guide leader's husband was travelling in Mexico
and every day visited a particular famous church where he
would sit and pray for me.

The woman who owned the salon where I worked, whose
children I also babysat occasionally, went to temple with her
whole family and, at the moment when the rabbi asked if
anyone had someone they wanted to pray for, they would all
say my name.

Someone brought me a small Buddha carved from stone
they'd bought in Nepal.

"A god is deciding this, not me," Alcestis says, but she later
contradicts herself: "I chose this! I did not have to choose it."

In her case it really was both: Death demanded a sacrifice, but Alcestis made the choice for the death to be her own. When I was working on the novel, there were many drafts in which Bea, in an attempt to take control of her life, took her own life. She didn't choose to get cancer, but she did choose how to live, which sometimes means how to die.

oo

I picked up a habit when I was young of trying to find
metaphors everywhere. When I look at something, I think
of how I could turn it into a metaphor. Waves become swans.
Swans become clouds. Clouds become islands.

"What do you think it looks like?" I ask Cal, pointing to
Lake Superior as we drive west along its north shore. The sky
is silver and the water is silver; the radio says a storm is
approaching. A vortex of clouds bends: it looks like liquid
metal; it looks like science fiction.

"It looks like a storm is coming over the lake," Cal says,
reminding me that sometimes it's good to just see a thing for
itself. Water is just water. Clouds are just clouds. The thing
itself can be enough.

∞

I find myself asking questions like "What does cancer want?" and "What is cancer's goal?" But, like us, cancer just wants to live. Like most living things, its goal is to be fruitful and multiply. In Siddhartha Mukherjee's history of cancer, he writes: "cancer cells are hyperactive, survival-endowed, scrappy, fecund, inventive copies of ourselves." And this, he notes, "is not a metaphor."

O

The third round was brief but intense: for five days, I was given chemo for twenty-four hours a day, which meant I was unable to ever leave the ward in case of spills, because only the staff on the eighth floor was trained in handling these extremely toxic drugs. I was also in the group room, which, as I'd noted, absolutely sucked. There were five patient beds and we weren't even separated by curtains. Any time an infusion of drugs or blood or saline ended, an IV beeped. Any time the tubing got blocked by an air bubble or a twist or even by someone sitting on it, which happened more often than you might think, an IV beeped. My nurses tried to placate me by saying being in the group room was a good sign: it meant I didn't have any contagious infections. This almost made me wish for an infection.

My mum wrote: *It is very hard to be in the group room. Noisy and chaotic.*

Every morning, my parents let me eat Lucky Charms and the extra sugar appeared in my urine. Worried about diabetes, the doctors made me switch cereals.

The list of all the foods I ate during those five days was extensive: after trial and error in the first two rounds, the nurses and doctors had come up with a rhythm of anti-nausea medication that worked against the chemo drugs. Pizza, take-out steak and potatoes from a restaurant on the other side of Nathan Phillips Square that my dad was able to run back to my room in "only nine minutes," Subway sandwiches, Doritos, "a mortadella sandwich at 10 p.m.," microwaved spaghetti Bolognese, peaches, plums, apples, Häagen-Dazs.

Families weren't allowed to use the patient bathrooms in the group room, and one morning my dad noted, not as a complaint but as a mark of pride, I think, that he woke up at five a.m. to be the first to use the parent shower facilities down the hall.

Six days after my admission, I was discharged—my shortest-ever time in the hospital. In my handwriting, on Saturday July 27:

Nurse Elizabeth says that I can have blood and chemo at the same time! Yay! This means I can leave earlier.

After discharge, though, unlike in the interlude between rounds two and three, I couldn't keep the infections away. My parents monitored me constantly, and as soon as my

temperature spiked, I had to go downtown. For three weeks
I bounced back and forth between home and the hospital,
being shuttled along the quiet midnight highway, radio off,
laying my head against the cool window.

JULY 30:

36.6

37.6

37.7

38.8 at 3am. Call to HSC.

38.6 at 4:15am at HSC emerg.

Naturally, my parents wanted me to be at home, for us to all
be at home together. I felt like I was betraying them, but that
wasn't what I wanted. I wrote on the forum during this period:

> When I'm at home, I'm worried about things more than I am
> in the hospital, because the doctors and nurses aren't there
> to notice things that can happen, but they still do. So it's
> a lot easier to be at the hospital.

Every time I returned to hospital with a fever, I had to be
admitted through the emergency room in order to have my
files processed and for a bed to be found for me somewhere.
Occasionally, especially if I wasn't receiving chemotherapy,
I would be placed in a general ward until room in the
hematology/oncology ward opened up.

And every time my dad and I returned to the emergency room, it seemed that same nurse was working, the one who spotted me on the first day and asked "Oncology?" The routine of this was comforting, something I could count on. The relief at not having to explain myself every time was immense, especially since sometimes the fellows or younger residents would need some training to become more sensitive to my situation.

One evening, a young medical intern I'd not met before asked me to breathe so she could listen to my lungs through her stethoscope—"deeper please, again, and again"—until I nearly fainted.

"You must have heard enough by now," I said. "I just can't breathe anymore," and I lay down, keeping my lungs to myself.

∞

The first person I loved told me *you are a miracle,* with such compassion and awe. But miracles are things we can't hope to understand. I feel desperate for some kind of understanding.

○

At some point in the summer—there is no note of his arrival in the notebook—a guy my age was admitted to 8A and given a room in the same corridor. It was rare to have teenagers on the ward—as it was a children's hospital, there were proportionately fewer of us in those upper years before the age cutoff. I'd only met two, and neither of them had ever been in-patients at the same time as me.

One of my nurses told me about the new arrival when she was checking my vitals. She said it as though it was exciting news. *A teenager. A boy.*

Owen had been flown in on a helicopter. His parents arrived a little while later, as they'd had to drive down.

Similar to dogs (*Fox, two years old, yellow-mouth cur*), there was a standard way that parents and patients summarized their situations in verbal introductions.

Harriet, fifteen, Richmond Hill, Natural Killer.

Owen, fifteen, Georgian Bay, Rhabdomyosarcoma.

Things I remember about Owen's arrival:

- He had a huge family, lots of siblings, and there would be cycles of large crowds that would drift around, aimless in the way that hospitals make you, usually congregating around the bench at the end of the hall.
- His parents were the same age as my parents.
- I knew that his situation must have been serious enough to fly him in with *Bandage 1*, the hospital helicopter, which landed on the rooftop.
- His flesh was so tightly packed to his bones and his skin had this waxen quality: it was yellow but also blue, as though his bare ankles, sticking out from underneath his hospital gown, were deprived of oxygen.

Accompanied by my parents, I went to Owen's room to say hello, and he said hello back.

∞

In my twenties I briefly dated a man who'd also had blood cancer in his teens. I'd never been with anyone with whom I could talk about that time in a way that acknowledged how it was something you could think about both all the time and not at all. A baseline. This man had been fifteen too, but not as sick as I was: he didn't have to spend nights in the hospital, and had been able to keep going to school.

When I told him about the novel version of the story I'd been writing, he said, "So Bea doesn't have boyfriends? You're making her out to be a kind of martyr, like a *Virgin Suicides* sort of thing?"

I didn't know how to respond. "No, she just doesn't think about it. I never dated anyone until years later, I just didn't think about it either."

My focus was on living. I didn't think about loving. Telling him about young Heracles, though, and how much attention he paid me, how often he visited me, how he would bring me gifts and ask if he could hug me, my date asked if this Heracles guy perhaps had been in love with me.

This was the first time I'd considered that. "I guess," I said, "that's possible."

This man had found the fiction unbelievable, but my explanation for it was that it was the truth. Maybe I just needed to write the truth, then.

OO

As soon as we make it to the Atlantic coast, I have to fly
back home for some doctor's appointments, including
what's called the "anatomy scan." The night before my
flight, as we have every night on our trip, we each write
a letter to the baby, whom we've been calling Bean. Cal's
handwriting is illegible even to him, so when it's his turn
he dictates, and I transcribe into the journal in which we're
collecting the letters.

"Dear Bean," he says, and I write. "Tomorrow your
mother leaves me and I will be alone with the two dogs.
At the end of the week, your mother will return to me and
you will no longer be a Bean but a she or a he in our minds.
You've always had a sex but this will be the first time that
we know it. I'm very excited for the ultrasound and very
curious, but more than anything, I'm excited to see your
little developing face for the third time."

Since ultrasound technicians are not allowed to disclose

any information, I have to wait for a call from my doctor's receptionist with the information, and she doesn't call me until I am inside the tube that attaches to the airplane, in line to board to go back to Halifax.

"Are you sure you want to know?" she says, "You don't want a surprise?"

I beg her, "Please just tell me."

She gives me the news and I immediately call Cal as I shove my bag into the overhead compartment and take my seat. I hadn't realized I was crying until he picks up the phone: suddenly the reality of this child's life is visible to me in a way it hadn't been before, and this is overwhelming.

Cal picks me up from the airport, and since he's a bit more reserved than the dogs, their enthusiasm for my return eclipses his. We drive mostly in silence—the rattle of the van on the highway in the wind makes it difficult to converse— heading for the valley near the Bay of Fundy. Every town we drive through has a sign saying *Highest Tides in the World Found Here!*

When we get to where we've decided to spend a few days, we set up camp in a mostly empty site. After heating up some soup and slicing bread for dinner, we get out the notebook where we write our letters to the baby, and Cal, again, goes first.

"I really missed your mother," he says, while I copy his speech and decide on appropriate punctuation based on his cadence. "But she was busy with appointments and seeing friends, so I had to live with that. I looked at some pictures of her to help."

I stop writing. "You missed me?" I ask. "You looked at pictures? You didn't tell me that."

"I knew I'd see you soon."

Cal continues to dictate his letter: "I was sitting by a lake in the woods when I got the call from your mother after she had her ultrasound, and I picked up a stone and scratched on a large rock the words: BEAN IS A BOY."

∞

October 17, 2017: The day is grey to wake up to but quickly grows sunny, increasingly warm, unaware of itself. I have coffee, eggs for breakfast, and bike over to Toronto General Hospital for an echocardiogram. In the journal, my dad wrote that I had one of these in those first few days, but I have no memory of that. One of the chemotherapy drugs in my protocol can cause damage to the heart over time, so mine has to be monitored.

I remember sitting with my parents and the pharmacist, a tall and bony woman with a Virginia Woolf face, going over every possible side effect of all of the many drugs I was being given. This was fifteen years ago. We were in a quiet room, clear, indirect daylight was filtering in through the window, and outside all I could see was more windows.

"This one can lead to eventual heart problems in some patients," she said. "Heart attacks, occasionally. But not until they're around thirty."

"Thirty?" My dad said. "But she's already fifteen."

To me, though, thirty seemed just as impossible as sixteen.

"Right," the pharmacist said apologetically, speaking above me. "Right. Most of the patients I deal with are only two. Thirty is much farther for them."

I am thirty now. I arrive at the hospital sweaty, though it's mid-fall and I'm not even wearing a coat. I've never been here before and find myself observing details. No, not observing, more like searching for details to try to find an anchor in the world, outside of myself. Tim Hortons in the lobby. Inuit prints on the walls. If I could collect enough facts, maybe I would feel less unstable. Facts are grounding.

I take a crowded elevator to the third floor and before I've even joined the lineup, a hospital worker, shorter than me, takes my health card: "Signing in? Just in time." He looks at me, and I think: What would have happened if I hadn't come? What would they have done? Would I have been lost in the system, rebooked for later? Could I find a way to avoid interference indefinitely? But I would never do this. This line of thinking is absurd to me. Disappearance is the highest form of anarchy. Everyone has to believe in something.

A receptionist confirms my birthday and emergency contact—my dad, it's always my dad's name that I write down instinctively, for he is the one who would come to clinic with me, who would update the records, who would distill the information and debrief my mother—and gives me a hospital bracelet.

DOB: 10/04/87. ADMITTANCE: 17/10/17

Cuffed. A different kind of anchor. I start to panic. It's an overreaction to give me a hospital bracelet with an admittance date on it for a one-hour outpatient procedure. It's an overreaction to panic, too, but one thing leads to another.

A hospital worker in different-coloured scrubs from the first introduces himself and guides me to the windowless imaging room. He tells me to remove my clothes from the waist up and put on a gown from the stack on top of the filing cabinet, keeping the string at the back open. He closes the shower curtain that divides the room and stands a foot away from me, on the other side of the burgundy fabric, as I disrobe. I started crying when the receptionist put the bracelet on me, but now my eyes are full-on leaking. I lie down on the bed, on the sheet of crisp paper. The sonographer asks if he can come in, and I apologize, which means yes.

He takes a seat on the wheelie chair in front of the machine, and gently directs me to come an inch towards him, face the wall, and take my left arm out of the sleeve. He lowers the lights. In the low light and with my body facing the wall, he cannot see the naked parts of me. This seems to be the intention behind the position, and I am doubly grateful because it also means he cannot see that I'm weeping.

He tells me that the gel is water-soluble, and that he will try to be gentle but sometimes the pressure needs to be a bit stronger in order to peek through the ribs.

I should tell him if I'm ever uncomfortable, though. He sticks three pads onto my skin, white with a small silver nodule to which cables attach, and this system monitors my heartbeat—that electric green dip/dip/climb you see on TV that peters out while the patient is in surgery. I want to watch the monitor just to make sure my line doesn't peter out, but I can't watch the monitor because I know I won't be able to look away if I do, longing to see something, not knowing what I'm reading, signs and symbols completely detached from one another.

Tears are coating the left side of my face now and I wonder if the machine can detect this level of emotion, whether my heart rate is jumping because of this. It's quickly becoming out of hand; my fear—is it fear?—is spiralling. I wonder if he knows. I don't think he knows.

There's a sign on the wall right in front of me that says NO PHOTOGRAPHS/VIDEOS/AUDIO RECORDINGS. SONOGRAPHERS ARE NOT ALLOWED TO DISCLOSE RESULTS. A CARDIOLOGIST WILL EVALUATE THE IMAGES. CALL YOUR DOCTOR TO REVIEW RESULTS.

He asks me if my doctor has ever told me he's heard a murmur, which seems to be disclosing the fact that he sees a murmur. Then he tells me that my "velocity" (I have velocity? A heart has velocity?) is normal. The machine pings every few seconds, every time he takes the measurements of something—the opening of a valve, the dimensions of a chamber. He tells me that the third bar on the screen (which I glance at quickly and then, as predicted, cannot look away from) is measuring the flow of blood.

He does all of these things despite the sign, so maybe he does know that I am crying. Maybe he is trying to be kind.

Crying, still crying, I try to focus on details in the room. More anchors. I notice the way that the cream metal bars of this stretcher-bed on which I lie cast shadows on the wall, even though the lighting is low, and remember a story I heard about how when blind children had their sight restored, they didn't understand the difference between light and shadow. They thought the shadows were solid objects and avoided the shady side of the street, thinking it physically obstructed by some unknown force. Maybe they're right; maybe they know something the sighted don't.

Crying, still crying, I try to pick apart my feelings and figure out what's making me sad, or scared, or whatever feeling it is that's making me cry. Naming the feeling can make it an anchor too, in its own way; naming something puts me in control of it, just like narrating does. I feel . . . I don't know. Vulnerable? Aware of my body as a fallible sack of flesh? Triggered by the memory of losing control of my body completely?

I cannot name it. It is beyond me. I am still crying.

My heart inside-out reminds me of a grapefruit that has been peeled. It is sacrilegious. But this metaphor doesn't work because grapefruits are not holy.

You know that feeling when you know you got the right answer, aced a test, understood why someone has been treating you a certain way even though they haven't explained it? This is what I'm after, lying on this cot. I can't get there.

After forty-five minutes the sonographer tells me he's finished, and that he has taken 102 pictures of my heart. I see one on the screen, and it doesn't look like a heart at all.

○

Owen was getting sicker. Owen never left the hospital. It wasn't my business, and nobody should have told me anything, but somehow I heard that the doctors just weren't finding the source of his tumour. The cells in his blood identified the cancer as a solid-tumour type found in the muscles, and he was being given chemotherapy to try to treat and shrink it, but they couldn't find the tumour to either operate or radiate.

I wanted to say something to him. I don't remember what I wanted to say to him, but I walked in there knowing I wanted to say something. I knocked on his door—unlike the medical staff, I always knocked—and a voice that sounded much stronger than he looked said "Come in." The lights were off in his room. His skin looked bluer. His limbs underneath the sheets reminded me of sand dunes.

I got a letter from one of my favourite nurses that night. I hadn't noticed that she'd come into his room to hang meds

from his IV, or start a blood transfusion, or whatever it was
she'd done. I was so concentrated on him, and without the
overhead lights on, it was shadowy in the corners of his
room. Her letter, which I still have, was handwritten on
a small piece of yellow paper, folded in half, with a flower
doodled on the front.

Dear Harriet,

I hope you don't mind that I overheard you talking to Owen
today, but I was in the room when you were speaking with
him, and I wanted to tell you how much it moved me. You
talked about bravery, and how he didn't need to be brave, he
just needed to not give up. You spoke with such grace and
compassion, I've never heard anyone talk like that, let alone
a patient of mine. You are a wonderful, inspiring young
woman.

xox, J

∞

The body experiences fear long after a threat has passed. Even if you're held up with what ends up being a toy gun, the rush of hormones and adrenaline are real, and will remain in your brain and bloodstream, temporarily overriding conscious thought so that the body can divert all of its energy to facing the threat. The fear is real even if it was triggered by something imagined.

If you're diagnosed with a fatal illness and then you survive, how long does it take for the body and mind to reconcile conscious thought with the disappearance of the threat? A lifetime, or less?

○

Round four of chemo started on August 19, after the infections and fevers had passed and my blood counts had become high enough to shoot back down. Here's what the first twenty-four hours looked like, according to my dad's notes.

DL & HL to clinic, before 8:30!! Finger poke 8:55am.
  Blood counts: 3.5, 111, 253, 117. Very good numbers.
  49.0 kg (108 pounds)
More peripheral blood taken at 10am, for checking clotting
  factors and need (or not) for Fresh Frozen Plasma. Saw
  JP in clinic.
10:20, Dr L for a look at HL, no need for FFP
11:30, Harriet hooked up to IV for glucose and saline.
  A room is available in 8A
12:40pm for BMA and LP (Bone Marrow Aspirate and
  Lumbar Puncture), out at 12:50

1:20, Morphine dose started in IV, and O2 sensor attached as well. To room 8 in 8A. Busulfan instead of radiation.

4:30, blue chemo started, only about ½ hour for it to run through. Once per day for 5 days. Anti-nausea drugs also.

5:15, Ara-C started. Twice a day for 3 days. 5pm and 5am.

5:20, Eyedrops given by DL, one drop per eye 4 times a day. Technique: HL flat on bed, eyes closed, drop fell on side of nose and ran into the eye.

Irene is nurse tonight.

Daisy was nurse today.

9pm, Harriet getting ready for bed.

Septra and Fluconazole tablets delivered and taken + one Tylenol for headache.

Asleep about 10:30 after story-time.

2am, temp normal

5am, Ara-C

Krista is our nurse today

Ondansetron running at 8:30am

Sleeping with earplugs meant that, for the story-time my dad notes, he had to speak loudly enough to go through the earplugs, sitting close by my side.

"You're yelling," I'd shout.

He'd adjust, then continue.

"Now I can't even hear you."

He'd adjust, then continue. In this near-nightly routine I put my parents through, neither of them ever expressed exasperation.

With the morphine drip, I was able to administer my own pain relief (to a degree: it maxed out at a certain point, though I was too nervous to ever get near that). I was told to punch the button whenever I hurt. This was my first time taking a narcotic so consistently, and it made me feel strange. The drug seemed to transform the world, rather than soften it—I didn't feel at home in the distorted reality it created.

The morphine pump is visible in a photo of me lying in a CT machine, one of my nurses standing next to me to funnel all of the tubing and monitor my vital signs during the procedure. In the photo you can see the top of my head, and I'm wearing a navy-blue bandana. I don't remember ever allowing bandanas. They felt like the equivalent of putting Band-Aids on an amputated leg. My hair, I haven't mentioned this, was thinning more dramatically by this point. The fact that I had held on to my hair for far longer than expected was a point of pride, but also enabled me to feel normal. If I looked normal, both to myself and other people, then I could be seen as normal. But now I was succumbing to the prognosis and this felt like a failure. Chemotherapy targets cells that divide and multiply quickly, targeting cancer cells but also hair follicles, and my body was obeying, rather than defying, the directive it was being given. This was the goal, and yet—

Looking again at the photo, I see my arms are up behind my head, extended on the infinite stretcher. There are probably thirty cords and tubes connected to me: the IV with its two blue pumps; an oxygen monitor on my index finger; and then some white tubes connecting me to what looks like an Easy-Bake Oven, a portable monitor to show the levels of my oxygen and blood pressure.

I wasn't allowed to move, and my body hurt. I had to hold my breath while the pictures were being taken in order to prevent even the subtle motions of breathing from blurring the image. There was an intercom in the machine, so I could hear when the technicians needed me to inhale, and then when I could let it go.

o

The conversation around my future fertility continued, still outside of my awareness.

August 20, my dad's handwriting:

> Toronto General Hospital does do ovarian surgery using keyhole method. Various ethical questions, in general. No successful pregnancies yet, in humans, after this procedure. Need to ask more questions of Dr. D. Procedure is still being done at Toronto General, for adults, in the hope of better technology for the future? Procedure is removal of one whole ovary, cold storage, then re-implantation after treatment is over.

As it was explained, this act was hopeless at present, but undertaken in hope for the future. I do remember being asked my thoughts on this, but I don't remember caring. I couldn't put my mind that far ahead.

I wonder what ethical questions were presented to my parents. I mean, we were already allowing the doctors to play God. Where do you draw the line?

The first successful pregnancies after this procedure occurred two or three years after I was presented with the option, and even today, ovary freezing and re-implantation is considered radical and experimental. But sometimes all you want is a chance—a reason to hope.

○○

At the obstetrician's recommendation, Cal and I sign up for "birth class" at the hospital where I've chosen to deliver the baby. I find the term hilarious. Nobody can *teach* you how to give birth; it just happens. Animals aren't taught, and they manage just fine. I learn that 251 babies are born every minute, and I bet most of the women giving birth to them have not taken a class to learn how to do so. The body, as always, knows what to do.

It turns out that birth class is mostly designed to make first-time parents aware of how what intuitively seems not normal is, in fact, normal. If your baby's hands and feet turn blue, that's normal. If your baby's whole body turns red, that's normal. If your baby poops green or orange, that's normal. What surprises me is the tour we take of the maternity wing. I have to hang back from the group and when Cal asks a question I nod and smile with my lips closed, knowing that if I open my mouth I will cry.

When we leave and enter the dark fall night, I finally burst: "it's just . . . a hospital!" I cry. We're walking through a garden of roses on our way home.

"I know that," he says. "Didn't you know that?"

"I guess," I say, trying to slow down, "but it just feels so much more . . . hospital-ish than I thought it would."

What I'd wanted was a beautiful hotel filled with medical staff and all the necessary emergency equipment present, but hidden. The rooms we've just seen look just like every hospital room I've ever been in. The same tubes and pumps, the same dingy fluorescent lights. The same smells, of antiseptic and microwaved meals. Even the same model of IV that I'd lived alongside fifteen years ago.

I want my baby born in a hospital because I know what can happen if things go wrong, but I want my baby born at home for the same reason: if things go wrong in a hospital, you lose control, and this time I haven't chosen to surrender.

○

Partway through the fourth round, I was discharged from
the hospital but the chemotherapy continued. My dad did
some brief training to learn how to flush and sterilize my IV
lines and then seal them with heparin, an anti-coagulant, so
that the lines would stay open to my bloodstream in case
I had to be hooked back up to the pump. The only chemo
I had to take was a pill, twice daily. My parents tried to
create a fairly normal rhythm for us, but this was hard. I was
throwing up all the time, had terrible headaches, and
couldn't sleep. I had prescriptions for several different kinds
of sleeping pills, but they didn't always work.

Four days after going home, my temperature spiked. My
dad drove me back down to the emergency room. I was
admitted instantly and underwent a litany of blood tests.
I felt myself spiralling. I was shaking, my jaw locked and
clattering, and I couldn't stop. In the journal, my dad
described this as a "spell of shivers."

Nursing note from my progress report:

August 28, 2010h, received pt awake shaking in stretcher
covered by blankets. Pt's face is pale + lips are blue. Pt said
"I'm cold."

There was a corridor. I was lying in a stretcher, being
pushed down it. I could see the beating of my own heart
through the skin of my abdomen, so strong it was making
my t-shirt bounce. The hallway lights were blue-tinted.
Someone asked me if I wanted anything to eat, and I said
blueberries. The nutritionist kept telling me I'd never put
on weight if all I ate was blueberries, but that was all
I wanted.

I was on my back, looking at the ceiling tiles as they
whizzed by above me, seeing their shapes morph and twist
and blur together.

"Do you see that?" I called my dad over and pointed to
my shirt. "My heart is beating too strong." Watching it only
seemed to make it go faster.

I closed my eyes. I couldn't look at my heartbeat
anymore, worried I would see it suddenly stop beating,
wondering how long it would take between me seeing it
stop and then not seeing anything anymore.

The nurse was called, she called one of my doctors, on
call and at home, and a different doctor came to look. My
dad wrote:

some discomfort . . . some anxiety . . . IV fluids had been cut down, Harriet seemed to be getting a bit dry, and the heart compensates by beating harder. So IV fluids increased.

Was that really all it was? I was just thirsty? How can you explain when something is more than just one thing?

The blood test results came back and I was told I'd contracted E. coli from my own gut. A compromised immune system can't fight off naturally occurring bacteria. My body didn't recognize itself. My body, once again, had turned against itself.

Mum's handwriting:

Nothing exceptional about H's condition, doctors said—just the patient is exceptional!

∞

Writing the journal was a way my parents were able to control the experience—to keep track of it, to put it into their own words. Writing this story as fiction was an attempt to take power over it, too. Does that mean that writing it as non-fiction is surrendering?

∞

I trusted that lightning wouldn't strike twice, and over time this came to feel like a kind of immortality. Ten years after I'd been living in remission, a young Australian resident doctor told me at my annual check-up that I now had the same likelihood of getting cancer as anyone else. My relief spilled over; I cried, crumpled; from then on, I let my guard down. I was given the opportunity to be ordinary, and my normal life was magnified, magnificent, when seen through the lens of the abnormal.

Two years after that, two events converged that made me realize I was not immortal at all.

1: My grandfather died. His death was expected; he was old, had been weary for years, and my granny often said how he would beg for death to relieve himself of the constant pain of living. But when his death actually came, I was stunned. I knew it was coming, I just never believed it would arrive.

2: The day after my granddad died, I was diagnosed with pre-cancer of the cervix. ("Pre-cancer" is such a strange term. The notion of pre-anything is odd, really, because it's a hypothesis, or a promise, rather than a state in itself. I remember walking through the quad of my small liberal arts college and hearing one guy say to his friend: "What does pre-law even mean? Why do you tell people that? I could just as easily say that I'm pre-banging your mom.")

I was in Amsterdam at the time and, unable to sleep, checked my email in the middle of the night. There was an email from my dad with the title "Letter from OHIP – for careful reading."

Hi Harriet,

A letter came for you today—so I opened it, later to find a notice 'to be opened by addressee only.'

All pages scanned and attached, in both English & French. We thought the French might be handy for follow-up there.

One letter, and 2 pages of Notes, in each language.

Please read carefully, and digest. No panic, but follow-up required.

Let us know if you want to talk over the options for follow-up.

Love from both of us

Dad

xx

I clicked the first of six attachments. "I want to thank you for taking the time to get a Pap test done. I am writing to let you know that your recent Pap test result is **abnormal**."

My first reaction was that "abnormal" meant that they hadn't obtained the right sample, not that the sample itself was abnormal. Which is incorrect. I continued reading: "these abnormal cells usually change back to normal on their own and are **almost never cancer.**"

Which party had decided to bold these words for emphasis? The doctors, or the communications specialists?

I was in bed beside my then-partner, still sleeping, and in the next moment I was out of the bed, on all fours, doing all I could to breathe. There was no reason for anyone to be awake at this time of night if they weren't already.

I'd already been through the *almost never*. I'd already come through the other side of *abnormal*. My body, it turned out, was still not on my side.

It broke my heart that my parents had been the ones to receive that letter, that they'd have discussed between them what this news meant, what they should do, how they should break the news to me. My dad's choice of words: "No panic." Not "don't panic," or "no need to panic." Written quickly, an attempt to be neutral maybe, or to encompass all three of us. No panic here. Nobody is panicking.

I was beyond panic. I was already at the point of giving up.

I wrote to a friend: "What's strangest is that, through the passing of the years and telling anecdotes about my experience, and writing fiction based on it, the whole leukemia thing seems distant and acceptable. I've rationalized it, and remember mostly feeling very strong and defiant. But when I read the letter, I realized that remembering myself as strong must be a coping mechanism of some kind, because I honestly don't feel strong at all right now, and that year, and many years following, truly were the worst experience I could possibly imagine, and thinking of having to go through it all again, well, I would simply rather not."

I was suddenly able to see that what had, at fifteen, felt inevitable—or at least like my only option—was more of a choice than I had realized. Back then, I'd chosen to remain blinkered and focus on the light. This time, I saw the barrel of the gun and I did not want to look away, or keep walking. Like passing an accident on the highway, I slowed down and couldn't stop staring.

∞

Awful things happen to good people for no reason, and we don't need to make logic of that. We are unable to make logic of that. But the opposite is also true. Look at the wildflowers blooming in the ditches, in the fallow fields. Spring blooms later the farther east you go, so as we headed to the Atlantic, Cal and I were following what felt like an eternally blooming spring as the baby inside of me grew from an orange to a cauliflower. I gathered armfuls of pink and purple lupins in the Maritimes.

Now, as we go west, and the baby grows to a cantaloupe melon: cornflowers along the shores of Lake Superior, anemones on the Assiniboine, salmonberries in the Rockies.

Reminders that the world indulges in beauty, too, for reasons that have nothing to do with us.

○

Plans were moving forward with the bone marrow transplant, though it was taking much longer than we'd all anticipated. A match had still not been found. At the end of that fourth round of chemo, it was decided that a fifth round should be added for safekeeping, a new development in the protocol.

My mum wrote on the forum on September 17:

The plan is that Harriet will be undergoing a 5th round of chemotherapy starting as soon as this Friday. In the absence of a donor the Drs want to give Harriet this 5th round to really consolidate the treatment and give them a chance to find a donor. If they do not find a perfect match they will not do a transplant, weighing up the side effects of a not-perfect match vs the chance of recurrence.

This next round has not been completed before by any patient at the hospital. The round will be 10 days and will be even stronger than the last. Harriet is barely recovered from

the last one and we had hoped that she would get a rest but
they want to test her bone marrow ASAP and proceed.

My dad wrote:

I don't understand what takes so long to find a match, what
with the speed of computers these days.

It did seem strange, as though there was some kind of old-
fashioned door-to-door campaigning going on in rural
villages. But the speed of computers has tricked us into
believing that there are always answers at our fingertips. We
think we can type our questions or desired locations into
a search bar and get a concrete answer instantaneously,
because this is what usually happens.

What's the temperature outside?

Will it rain today?

How far to the moon?

What is the etymology of cancer?

What is a Natural Killer cell?

Will this kill me?

If not this, then what?

I felt as though my life depended on the discovery of this
person who had matching bone marrow to mine,
somewhere in the world.

∞

I want this to be a book not about cancer, or even motherhood, but about *becoming*.

We see Alcestis in the process of dying, and then we see her in the process of coming back to life: Heracles brings her back in this in-between state, saying she won't be completely herself for three days.

Unless we are dead, we are in a state of becoming. And even then, perhaps *becoming* is another way of saying *surrendering*.

As I move away from one and towards the other, I am still the girl, and I am still death: both elements are, forever will be, within me.

∞

It's November 16, 2017, and the point of today is receiving a Facebook message from Megan's mother.

> Hi Harriet. I know this is totally random but my daughter was a patient at sick kids at the same time as you. We are here today for our follow up apt and I thought of you and thought I'd look you up. Glad to see you are doing well. My daughter Megan had leukemia too. She is in remission as well. I just wanted to say hi and let you know I was thinking of you, even tho you probably don't remember me! Take care!

I click on this woman's profile, find Megan, and recognize her instantly. Her huge, spoon-like blue eyes and broad forehead. Her curly hair—it's brown now, but the kind of brown where you can tell she'd been blonde as a baby.

Hi! That's crazy. I do remember you and actually tried to look
up Megan on Facebook recently, but didn't have any
information to go on. There are a lot of Megans. I'm so glad
to hear she's doing well. She must be nearly 17 now right?

How is it possible that even though I'm sitting on my
sofa, a half-empty cup of cold coffee on the table, the dogs
curled up and sleeping at my side, I'm also in the dark
bedroom across the hall from mine, an eighteen-month-old
baby holding herself up in a playpen, her forehead sticky
with sweat gone cold?

Megan is sixteen now, and posts memes about pot and
selfies where she's smoking bongs. Her mother says she
doesn't remember anything about being in the hospital,
"which I guess might be a good thing."

She is in remission as well. Remission is a state of not-
having-cancer. It is a tenuous state: "a temporary diminution
of the severity of disease or pain." Perhaps this is true of
Megan's state and my own. Perhaps it is the state of everyone
not currently dying.

Megan's mother caught me up on her daughter's life in
shorthand, the kind of headlines that you'd give to an old
family friend. Megan has epilepsy as a result of the
chemotherapy. I wonder if that is a result of treating the
tumours behind her eyes, since epilepsy was never raised
with me as a possible side effect. Megan's sister, nineteen
years old now, has two children. "She's a bit young for it, but

they are a blessing either way." *Blessing.* I wonder if she is religious, and how that would be possible.

She says she split up from the girls' father shortly after Megan left the hospital, and she implies the relationship didn't end well. I feel a space open up for me to tell her about the conversation he had with me, and type it out in a rush, clicking *send* before a second thought.

"Yeah. He's not a very good person," she writes back. "I'm sorry you had that experience with him."

My parents don't remember that conversation—maybe I never told them—and the acknowledgement feels better than the apology.

o

In the drama program at my high school, all of the students from all four grades went on a three-day retreat every September to a camp property on a lake a few hours north. There were talent shows and group cuddles, campfires and midnight hikes. No makeup or hair products were allowed, in an attempt to bring everyone onto a more equal plane. The girls not being allowed to wear concealer and mascara was no more dramatic, in the early 2000s, than the boys not being allowed to gel their hair.

That September I was technically in grade ten, but I hadn't actually entered school or done any work. The retreat fell in between my fourth and fifth rounds of chemo, and I was well enough to leave the hospital, so my dad took me up to the camp for an afternoon.

The first picture is of my friends all around, but not touching me, as I get out of the car. My teacher from *Alcestis* the year before is standing slightly farther back, taking a photograph. (I overheard him remind people that I needed my space, and to try to act normal around me.)

I'm wearing flared jeans, Adidas shoes with pink stripes, and a gauzy mauve shirt with a turquoise flower on the front. I'm carrying a black purse over my shoulder in which I keep Purell and lip balm. My limbs so rangy I'm positioned like a classroom skeleton. My wig, I think, looks pretty natural. In one photo, I've even put my sunglasses over it, like when you just slide up your glasses over your forehead when the sun goes behind a cloud and the world darkens—though in my case, that action would have been anything but second-nature: it would have involved delicate placement and rearranging, worrying whether I'd shifted the wig.

The photos from that day show a large group of us, fifteen or so, sitting on the dock; then eating popsicles on a dirt path; then standing by the point on the cliff over-looking the pines and the bashed-pewter lake. In every photo, young Heracles is standing just behind me, like a bodyguard. The last photo is dusky, the grain pixelated. Most of the people are laughing, pushing each other, arms tangled up, but I'm sitting slightly off to the side, smiling so hugely, hands to myself and dark circles under my eyes. With my eyelashes and eyebrows disappearing, the darkness stands out more dramatically. In contrast with the rest of these people, healthy, normal people who'd spent a summer in the sunshine, my pallor—especially in the twilight—is truly luminous.

OO

Weeks before my due date, my mother starts preparing and freezing meals for Cal and me to eat in the early days of new parenthood. She bakes dozens of muffins and scones, makes giant batches of curry and chili and soup. We have to tell her to stop when our freezer can't fit any more Tupperware.

My dad builds a mobile out of things from the hardware store. On the bottom of the wooden structure he inserts a hidden pocket between two slats of plywood where he places a note: "When the mobile is no longer needed, all parts can be re-used as originally intended."

My parents' love of nourishing me is renewed, knowing that I am nourishing another.

∞

After receiving the letter from Cancer Care Ontario about my cervical cells, I called my hippie family doctor to ask what to do. He didn't use the word cancer, but told me to get a follow-up test in Paris, where I was living, to see if the cells had disappeared, stayed the same, or developed.

I obeyed.

When I received the news that they'd developed, I was alone in my apartment. It was too early to call any of my doctors back home, so I Googled "cancer care help-line." My screen was blurry through tears so I clicked the first one I saw. It just happened to be in Ireland.

The woman who answered was so kind and patient that it made me cry even harder. I explained my situation through sobs, and she listened intently. After a minute, she said, in her lovely lilting accent, "Let me just get this straight. Are you Irish?"

"No," I wailed.

"And do you live in Ireland?" she said, still the pinnacle of kindness.

"No!"

"Right, well, I'm not sure what it's like in France," she said, "but this is what I would tell you if you lived in Ireland . . ."

Of all the people I spoke with before and after the procedure to remove the lesions, she was the most helpful. We even corresponded via email for a few days afterwards. The condition is a fairly common one; they removed the lesions successfully, and though I'll have to monitor it, there's no reason to believe further treatment will be necessary.

But the most difficult thing to wrap my mind around was the fact that I had been wrong: lightning is indiscriminate. Lightning will strike however many times it likes.

○

My dad's handwriting:

Tings and Bianca trying to figure out how to do a
new special sample extraction from the back of the throat,
via a nasal tube (?!) and negotiation led to a WOW bead
for this.

My mum's handwriting:

Delicious casserole from Christine for our dinner.

The "wow" bead I received in exchange for this procedure
was a large, plastic, patterned bead to go on my string of
"Bravery Beads," a program run by volunteers at the
hospital. Consider them more like "Event beads," in which
a red bead is given for every blood transfusion, a star for
each X-ray or CT scan, a teddy bear for being in isolation.

I had almost a hundred red beads, for example. Kids would generally hang them from their IV poles, and as we all trundled around the ward, we could visualize each other's timelines: the longer you'd been there, the longer your string.

∞

I never talked to my parents about what they believed in, but recently I asked my dad about God. He thought about it for a while, and then said: "I think God can be a useful concept for children."

O

Before the fifth round, my mum took me to a strip mall in Markham to get acupuncture, but I refused to have any more needles. Seeing even these ones, wispy, almost decorative, made me feel faint. So the man performed "acupressure," using his thumb and index finger to press certain points on my body. He wore grey sweatpants. He squeezed either side of my upper right knee.

"This part"—he looked at me, then at my leg—"when I put pressure right here, it makes the cancer cells disappear."

"Right," I said, hating him. Did he know he was lying, or did he really believe what he was saying? If what he said was true, I thought bitterly, wishing myself out of that window-less room, he wouldn't be working out of a strip mall in Markham and I wouldn't have been through this many months of chemotherapy.

A little while later, I saw a book called something like *The Spiritual Root of All Illnesses* in the waiting room of a massage clinic. I flicked through it to find "Cancer: Leukemia," which was said to be caused by self-hatred as a result of feeling rejected or misunderstood by one's mother.

I wish I'd thrown the book out and left the clinic, but all I did was put it back at the bottom of the pile and continue waiting.

○○

We are driving west through the prairies when I ask Cal
whether he thinks we should freeze the baby's stem cell–rich
umbilical cord blood in a private or public bank—that is,
whether we should keep it for ourselves, to use for our own
child later, or donate it to the public system to be used
whenever, and for whomever, it might be required. There are
crayon-yellow canola flowers on either side of us, on every
side of us. People talk about how shocking it is to be in such
flatness, but I am surprised by how comfortable, how at
home, it makes me feel. If you live in a place where you're
always able to see where you came from and where you're
going, would that change things?

"Does our child have a higher chance of getting
leukemia?" Cal asks.

He asks this as though he hadn't considered the question
before, as though its significance is irrelevant, and I love him
for this: it implies that we are doing this no matter what, that

there's no sense worrying about tragedy before any sign of it appears, and that if it comes to that, then we will get through it together.

"No," I say, "I asked my doctors, and it isn't hereditary."

The sun is behind a curtain of cloud, and the dogs are sleeping in the back of the van. The landscape makes me feel comfortable, but I should also mention that there are treacherous winds and tornado warnings; eight tornadoes have already touched down near the southern border, so we have checked the map and are on a more northerly road.

I scan the horizon and see no threats.

"Then let's go public?" he suggests.

I agree.

o

One of my primary doctors, Dr. L, was both extremely mild-mannered and extremely slender. The combination of her meek temperament and long, narrow bones gave the impression she might dematerialize. I was one of her first patients, and she understood that I was curious and involved. One day, when I was feeling well enough, she allowed me to look through a microscope at my own cells, the dark maze of my DNA. She brought me into a small room I'd never noticed before—right next to the room where I was anaesthetized for bone marrow aspirates and lumbar punctures—and had my blood ready between two clear plastic plates. There's a photo of me in profile at a desk, looking into the black monocular tube; my eyes are wide open, my eyelashes almost gone. I almost expected to feel some kind of possessiveness, a recognition, in seeing my own cells. I didn't, though. I looked at them with the reverence I feel for all science, all truth, all mysteries I don't understand. I thought: there is something powerful there that I am so close to, and yet will still never know.

∞

A paper about my case was published in 2005. One of my primary doctors recently sent it to me. There are pictures of my chromosomes and magnifications of my cancer cells. It starts:

"A 15-year old female presented with subconjunctival bleeding associated with cough. She related a history of fatigue, weight loss, and malaise over the preceding several months. Physical examination demonstrated pallor, bilateral subconjunctival hemorrhages, splenomegaly, and generalized lymphadenopathy."

Symptoms: the bleeding under my eyes, the swollen spleen and liver that had caused me to pee the bed, swollen lymph nodes. Funny to think of *malaise* as a medical term.

"Blasts were positive for the myeloid markers CD33 (97%), HLA-DR (99%), and CD11b (66%). Blasts were also positive

for CD4 (99%) and CD56 (99%), which are markers
associated with monocytic and natural killer leukemias . . .
Immunophenotyping by flow cytometry showed that the
blasts had a unique immunophenotype, which was not
typical of any recognized entity of leukemia."

Seeing myself in the abstract, written in the cool third-
person neutral of a medical journal, feels more like looking
in a mirror than I'd have anticipated. This is the recognition
I was looking for.

○

The same doctor who told me that in his religion people get sick as a punishment told my mother that the reason I was still alive was due to love. Though I don't remember him being there, he told me that he was one of the doctors who first saw me in the emergency room, blood in my eyes and bruises on my face. He said that he hadn't thought I'd make it.

"Only 50 per cent of your daughter's survival can be attributed to the medical profession," he told my mother, "and the rest of her survival is due to your family, your love and positivity."

I can forgive him this, knowing that my mother considered his words a rare gift, but his comments cause me physical pain. All of the patients I met were loved.

○

Owen was still there. The doctors still hadn't found the source.

In my novel, there was a boy Bea's age whom she would go visit. She was sleeping when he died, in the middle of the night, and nobody would tell her what had happened. The book was called *Everything We Could*. I liked that there was hopefulness to this phrase in one context—"it was everything we could have imagined!"—but that it's also what doctors say, what the doctors said in the story, when people die.

"I'm sorry," they'd say, taking off their tiny glasses, the heart rate flatlining on the monitor. "We did everything we could."

O

On September 20, we were told that a bone marrow match had been found. We knew nothing about the donor, but I instantly and forever after imagined it was a man, about twice my age, and living in England. The match was a 9/10, which was extremely good, they said. The closer the match, the less likely my body—"the host"—was to be attacked by the donor cells, or "the graft." Graft versus host disease is one of the most serious risks of any kind of transplantation, but it's most commonly associated with bone marrow transplants.

Most animals do not carry their young within their bodies for the same reason: one would reject the other, and there would be no survivors. If it weren't for a virus which led to the formation of the placenta, mammals as we know them would not exist. Mother mammals develop this organ in order keep the blood and waste separate from their own bodies while growing their young. Among other things, this is why our children can have different blood types than us, different DNA, different everything. Because of a virus, children start out life, as Alcestis said, as "masters / In their own house," even though they are housed within our bodies.

∞

In my twenties I volunteered in the cancer ward of a children's hospital in Paris, and met a young boy, about fourteen years old, who wanted to practice his English with me.

"Sure," I said, delighted to feel like I had a real reason to be there—most of the time I wandered the halls feeling useless. "What do you want to talk about?"

"Anything."

"Okay, do you like books?"

"Not much."

"Movies?"

"Not much."

The feeling of uselessness was creeping back; these were mostly all the things I talked about. "What about sports?"

"I like sports," the boy said.

"Great."

Silence.

"I like to go running," he said.

"I like running too!" I replied, overly elated.

This boy and I figured out that we lived in the same neighbourhood in Paris, on opposite sides of the most beautiful, wildest park in the city.

An expression of nostalgia came across the boy's face, and in the moments before he spoke, I could see he was inhabiting a beautiful memory. "When I had health," he said, in his accented English, "I would go running in the park of the Buttes-Chaumont."

When he *had* health. When health was something he possessed.

I didn't tell this kid that I'd had cancer too. I didn't want to take anything away from his own experience. Every time I run now, I think of this boy. I have health, so I run.

∞

I've been thinking a lot about permanence. When the surgeons told me, before inserting the central venal catheter into my jugular, that a scar would remain on my chest, I didn't think about for how long. I wasn't thinking about forever then. But it will never not be there. Forever is impossible to fathom. For until I die.

My friend in Sweden had a baby and wrote to me when he was five weeks old, five weeks before my baby's due date: "the realization that the baby is here with me for (hopefully, if God is good) the rest of my life has taken me somehow unaware. Forever is so definite, and the thought of the responsibility is sometimes frightening—he is so small and helpless and in need of protection—and if anything happened to him, how would one survive?"

This friend and I both used to model for a painter friend of ours called Rosy. There's a particular painting of Rosy's that's always been one of my favourites: my friend is lying on her side, breasts and belly facing us, with a grey cloth—which always reminded me of a void, rather than a blanket—over her hips and legs. Her eyes are downcast and she looks mournful, nearly wounded, and yet simultaneously deeply at peace. I asked my friend what she was feeling while it was being painted, and she laughed: "That painting took months, I was thinking so many things!" This was before I started modelling myself.

The first time I posed for Rosy, she asked me to get onto a table topped with a mattress and find a comfortable position. I lay on my stomach and crossed my arms underneath my head. "Perfect," she said. "That's perfect, just like that." She got a permanent marker and drew circles to mark the feet of the table as well as her easel, so that the perspective would remain constant. She also used masking tape to mark my elbows, head, hips, and feet, as well as the edge of the pillow I held. Any time I took a break, or when I returned for the following session, it was important to find just the same pose again.

It was such a comfortable position, and such a comfortable situation, that I often fell asleep as she painted me. When I was awake we would talk, but when she was working on my face we didn't talk, and I would watch her face at work.

While she paints, her face gets so worked up with concentration that it almost looks as if she is labouring to build something physical. A house, not just a painting. She's constantly looking at me—in a way that feels like she's looking through me, like I am object, subject, background and foreground, but already just a painting—and putting the paintbrush at various angles to compare the lines of my body to the straight line of the brush.

I like watching the colours she picks up and wondering to which part of me they correspond, but it's almost impossible to guess. What I've learned is that human skin, flesh, is made up of every colour, really.

Though it's a matter of fact that having your portrait painted captures you, the subject, at a particular and transient moment, I never thought of it that way. I didn't think about it being a past record in a distant future because modelling, for me, is a way of spending time in the present. Like being on a train, modelling is a way for me to stay still and yet be doing something. Going somewhere. Thinking about things. Getting transformed into art.

I returned to Rosy's studio once or twice a week over the course of a spring and summer as she worked on that first painting. I went to Switzerland and got a tan, which meant she had to darken the colour of my skin; I got my heart broken and then fell in love, which probably changed nothing about the painting for most people, but when I look at it, I know. Rosy requested I wear little or no makeup but keep my nails painted the colour they had been the first day: she loved the pale oceanic blue and thought it worked well with the overall colours and feeling of the painting. The name of the nail polish was "Sea Change," and the name of that painting is just *Harriet*. Rosy started *Harriet* when she was three months pregnant, and finished just before she gave birth.

Right after the pre-cancer had been found in my cervix, I told Rosy about how I had, as if for the first time, realized that I would one day die.

"Oh, of course," she said, immediately understanding. "That's the greatest fear. But isn't it just so amazing to be alive in this moment?"

○

Round five started on September 24. The chemotherapy was scheduled to start at four p.m., and at two o'clock, my mum noted that *we went to sing Happy Birthday to Richard. He is 4 today.*

The little boy's mother was speaking to my dad, cycling through the futile litany of "why me, why us, why him." Later, my dad went back to their room and took the mother aside.

"This kind of thinking," he told her, "you just can't go there. It's not worth it. It won't help your son. You have to work so hard to be positive, for him if not for yourself."

I didn't know my dad had done this until years later. My mum told me. She said he did the same for her.

○

Partway through the fifth round, we had a conversation
with the doctors about whether or not to continue with
the bone marrow transplant. My dad wrote: *BMT should
be a fresh start*, to which I added *and is what they recommend*.
My parents were wavering on whether or not a transplant—
an incredibly risky procedure that would guarantee a more
difficult life in the long term, even if it did work—was
a good idea, but I no longer trusted my own body.
I wanted a new one.

   That night, a note from my mum: *3:30am, spaghetti
dinner!* Behind these two words is a much bigger moment.

   It's hard for my mum to talk about this period. Usually
she finds a way to avoid the subject, or talks instead about
the generosity and support we received as a family back
then. She had to work harder than my dad did to put on
a brave face for me; I never saw her cry back then, yet
I knew it happened when I wasn't around. But today I ask

her bluntly, over the phone, if she was ever afraid that
I would die.

"Do you remember," she says to me now, her in her
home and me in mine, "one night, when I was on duty at
the hospital, you called out at three a.m. and asked if I was
awake?"

I tell her I don't remember this.

"I said I was awake, and you said, in a quiet voice,
'Mummy, am I going to die?' and in my head I was
screaming," she starts crying over the phone, finally letting
down the wall she'd erected to protect me from her fear,
"I was so terrified, that's what I was so worried about and
thinking all the time, but out of my mouth came the words
'of course not, don't be silly, you are what makes Dad and
I a family and nothing is going to change that.' And then
you were quiet for a moment and said, 'Okay, I'd like some
spaghetti, please.'"

She wrote about the food but she remembered the fear.
She had been my first home, she felt responsible for keeping
me safe in this world, and I wonder if, in these moments,
she felt she had failed.

And so, at 3:30 a.m., my mum made me a microwaved
spaghetti dinner on the china she had brought from home.

∞

I text my friend:

Two questions
    If I buy a giant container of blueberries can I freeze some?
Like, is frozen fruit just fruit that is frozen? Second question:
do you ever get such an overwhelming sadness just that time
is passing?

I lived in New York for a summer, after graduating from
university and before moving to Paris. Going back to New
York to visit, six years after I'd left, I saw a guy I'd known
when I lived there, and whom I hadn't seen since.

"Hey," he said. "It's been a while! You still living at the
corner there?"

I was stunned. It had been six years. Did he honestly
think I could have lived there for that long without us
having crossed paths? Was it that his sense of time was

completely distorted, and he didn't realize how long it had been? Or was he just making polite chit-chat?

I lived in Paris for seven years and have now been living in Toronto for two. Just now, as I was walking on the rail path in my neighbourhood, a guy went past me on a skateboard, and he looked just like a neighbour I'd had in Paris. This neighbour was a fixture in my life: not important in it, just contextual. I have not thought of him in years, but when this guy who was not my old neighbour skated past me, I felt a shortness of breath and tears in my eyes. I have new neighbours; I will never have that man as a neighbour again. Or at least, not in the same place, the same time.

My friend responds:

1. That's a googler but I'd say yes
2. Of course. That sadness is a gift so you don't miss the passage of time.

The past, though we carry it with us always, is untouchable.

○

The chemotherapy was doing its job battering down blood cells, and I was a bystander taken down in the wake of the drugs. I got extremely sick. More sick than I had really ever been up until then.

On October 8, I wrote on the forum:

Hellooooo 😀

The doctors have confirmed (sort of) that this infection is the same one as last time—as well as a few more 😔 😫, so they are discussing taking out my Central Line and replacing it after a few days of antibiotics, since the infection could be IN the Ivy line 😔. I'll have to have 2 surgeries though, one to take this line out, and then a separate one after a few days of antibiotics to put another line in. I had a chest Xray today to make sure that I don't have pneumonia (which I don't 😎) and the doctor let me see it! It was really cool, you can see the Central line in my chest!

I was started on a two-week-long course of four different aggressive antibiotics for an infection for which they did not know the source, and the cause of which would likely not clear up until my immune system recovered.

Before the surgery to remove the central line, I spent an entire day NPO waiting—no food or liquid all day—and receiving blood transfusions to get my numbers higher for a safer surgery. At 11:15 p.m., the surgery was called off because my counts were wavering and the operating-room schedule was still just too full. Exhausted and frustrated— and in my case, starving—my dad and I ordered pizza.

The surgery was finally performed the next day, a Saturday.

October 12, my dad's hand:

> 38.4 Celsius at 12:15 am, Tylenol
>> Kirsten on duty again. More platelets planned to get closer to 100 for OR.
> 9:45am, the call we've been waiting for—HL to OR
> 10:00, platelets started
> 10:15, down in OR (whole bed moved from room 21).
>> Dr. Eger is the surgeon. "Snowman suit" for DL to be with HL 'til she had the sleepy milk at 10:45.

I wonder if "sleepy milk" was the hospital's term or my father's. I don't remember hearing it, but the anaesthetic was a thick, white milky liquid that, if put through a peripheral

IV in my arm rather than the permanent IV in my chest, burned like a punishment for the brief seconds that I was awake to feel it. I suppose it still burned after I was knocked out.

Later that night, in my mother's hand:

5pm, Mary arrives with apple pie and Mummy's
   Minestrone Soup.
Harriet told us of incident in recovery room when nurse and
   anaesthetist were discussing Harriet's case, thinking she was
   asleep. We told Kirsten and the nurses on 8A called and
   spoke to the nurse in OR, who was v. apologetic and upset
   and said she would talk to the Dr. and not do this again.

Trying to remember this is like trying to remember a dream from half a life ago. I'm not sure I can pin it down. What comes to me is something between images and feelings. There were so many dark hospital rooms, the sense of an abyss always before me, strangers all around me, a solid wall at my back with medical supplies affixed to it, a blood pressure cuff and oxygen tanks. These were the constants, no matter where I was. As I try to recall this particular moment, overhearing this conversation as I was coming out of the fog of anaesthetic, I have a sense of solidity coming out of the shadows, I have a feeling of being very small, but still, all I see are shadows.

When I ask my dad about this moment now, he immediately looks concerned. "Oh yes, you were very upset," he says. "I wasn't allowed to be with you when you woke up because they were monitoring your breathing, and when they finally let me in the room, you were still quite foggy but very upset about what you'd heard: one nurse asking another what it was that you had, and upon hearing what it was, saying something like 'Oh, I wouldn't wish that upon anyone,' or something. It wasn't malicious, but they shouldn't have said that around you."

I tell him that the note in the book said it was a nurse and an anaesthetist, and he says, "Oh, well it was a long time ago. Perhaps." This detail may be blurred, but his memory of my feelings, and their consequences, is sharp.

Even though I didn't—and still don't—remember this moment, I did incorporate something about this into the novel. My memory of the reality has merged with how I wrote about it.

In the book, Beatrice is awake in her room at night, her mother asleep on the cot at her side, and she hears two nurses discussing whether or not she's aware of just how sick she really is.

"They think it's the Natural Killer?" one nurse says.

"Poor girl," the other responds.

As a fifteen-year-old, a minor, I was a subject of my parents. It was up to them to tell me what they thought I should know, and I felt that I was aware of everything. Maybe there were gaps in what I was told, but there were also spaces in what the doctors knew, and in how we were able to comprehend their information. (*There is a crack in everything / that's how the light gets in.*)

But when Bea heard these two nurses, it was the first time she'd heard the term "Natural Killer," and she learned that her condition was far more serious than she'd been led to believe.

O

The surgery to remove my central line didn't take away the infection. The fevers continued. In addition to the new permanent IV on the inside of my left bicep, which has left me with a scar shaped like a star, a second peripheral IV was inserted so that I could have more drugs simultaneously. A rash, or just an itch, developed on my upper cheek, near my left eye. A nurse noticed it, told a doctor, and that same afternoon a dermatologist came to take a skin sample from the patch of skin that required two stitches to close and morphine for the pain, and left me with another tiny scar.

Nothing was ever found from this skin sample. It was probably just a pimple. I knew they were getting desperate.

The "if she starts shaking" drug was started up again. The nurses changed its name from amphotericin to amphoterrible. This time, I did start shaking. A lock-jawed, full-bodied, fever-dream tremor.

1:15am: Rigors from ampho. Given Demerol.

3am: Rigors again. Given more Demerol.

It felt like my rib cage was closing in, my lungs aching from the squeeze. I loved the Demerol, though. It made my whole body melt and all pain go away. At one point it was noted that though I had "no real rigors, H thought she needed Demerol to avoid them."

More tests: I had to drink radioactive liquid called "contrast" in order to make my intestines show up more brightly in a CT scan, and it made my pee burn. I was told I'd need a third IV inserted into my foot so that they could give me more blood transfusions, but when my nurse saw me panic at this prospect, she convinced the doctors to just wait an hour and she would find a way to use an IV I already had, flushing the potassium infusion with a bolus of saline in order to clear the lines.

No conclusive results came from this scan either.

Two weeks after the antibiotics began, my fever was still uncontrollable and spiking every few hours, as soon as the Tylenol wore off. The drugs were wearing me down. The doctors needed to find the source of the infection in order to obtain a clear sample of what it was so that I could be treated more effectively.

Another procedure: a bronchoscopy was ordered to biopsy a few cloud-like patches appearing in my lungs, and this would need to be done under another general anaesthetic.

A bronchoscope would be inserted down my throat to pass through my trachea and scissors would be attached to the camera so that the sample could be snipped and extracted.

My throat hurt for days afterwards. This biopsy, too, provided no conclusive results.

They tried hormone injections, blood transfusions, new antibiotics, a new pump added to my IV to distribute more drugs, pain relief administered with stick-on patches—like a nicotine patch—so as to free up the IV lines. More fevers, more rigors, more vomiting.

Retreating, the doctors considered their next plan of attack.

oo

Is it too "on the nose" to point out to you that I was sick for nine months, the same amount of time that it takes to gestate a baby?

For the first few weeks, both cancer and the baby are silent, invisible; there are felt sensations but they are slippery, not to be trusted.

In both illness and pregnancy there is a sense that my body is not wholly, exclusively mine. My body has been occupied. *Occupy* is a metaphor used in war, which is what comes to mind first, but what I mean is closer to tenancy. I mean inhabited more than I mean dominated. My body is the house.

After giving birth, many mothers experience a feeling of loss, of their own selves being split and divided. This seems intuitive to me. I can see how easily I could slip from that sensation into something deeper. A friend sends me an article on recommended supplements to take to prevent what's called "the baby blues": tryptophan, tyrosine, blueberry extract, and blueberry juice.

"You'll just have to shovel blueberries down all day," she says. "Doesn't sound so bad."

○

Brought gift for Owen's family but he had passed away.

Beneath that line, my mum wrote his family's last name and
home address—that must have been given by one of the
nurses, though I know that's not allowed.

And that was it. Owen was dead. His name was wiped off
the patient whiteboard near the nurses' station, and his
family had no reason to ever come back to the hospital. The
doctors had found the source of the tumour too late, and it
was inoperable: the muscle-based solid cancer appearing in
his blood was blossoming behind the hardest-working
muscle in the body—his heart. I don't remember learning
any of this information, I just remember knowing it.

I Google Owen now, along with the town where he
lived, and find a picture of his gravestone. He died four
months before his seventeenth birthday. His gravestone,
pink quartz, has an engraving of Terry Fox, mid-run, and

along the bottom is written, "Absent From The Body, Present With The Lord."

It's one of those gravestones with a picture on it, an oval-shaped colour photograph—his school portrait. He has a wonky haircut and is wearing a Tommy Hilfiger t-shirt. "Beloved Son," the gravestone says. He looks so young in the picture, younger than I remember him being, although realistically it's probably the last school photo he was present for, so he must have been at least fifteen. I can see now, though, that he was just a child. We were just children. I haven't seen his face for over fifteen years and wouldn't recognize him, then or now. His face, in my memory, is always in shadow, and blurred into fiction, into the many ways I tried to reconcile his presence and absence in writing. In the novel I was writing, his death was a catalyst for Bea's death: when he died, she realized for the first time that death was a possibility.

○○

Lately Cal and I have been debating the idea of souls. He doesn't believe in them; I'm desperate to convince him. I think what I want is for him to agree that the baby inside of me is more than just a random collection of cells. I feel a deep urgency that there be acknowledgement, a universal agreement, that something must be greater than the self. This desire runs parallel to my need to believe that it wasn't just me, or my parents, or any one of my doctors, who was the bottom line on whether or not I lived or died.

We're spending the night near Little Manitou Lake, the only salt-water lake in Canada, a place where Indigenous people have been bringing their sick for centuries. The campsite is overcrowded, but when I walk into the lake and float, I am the only person in the whole body of water. I lie on my back, my belly rising like a moon over the waterline.

I try a kind of cheap Socratic method. "Am I different from you?" I call to Cal, who is sitting on the sand at the shoreline. He doesn't like to swim.

"Yes," he agrees.

"And is Fox different from Disco?"

"Yes, but—"

"Can't we call those differences *souls*?"

When I say "soul" what I mean is a kind of animating force: life, I guess. The word comes from the Greek *to breathe*. Breathing life into clay, the touchstone of so many creation myths. The word smacks of godliness, though, and of all the justice and retribution that go along with that. The everlasting soul is what that doctor believed was being punished.

The water is so cold but I'm already used to it. I stand in the shallows and feel the baby move, maybe his arms, maybe his legs; I can't picture his body inside of mine. I read a pamphlet at the campground that explained how, when smallpox was ravaging the Cree and Assiniboine Nations around this lake, the sick migrated towards the shores and bathed in the water.

More vehemently atheist than I am, Cal comes to agree, or at least I can get him to concede, that life is a soul, and as long as we are alive, our souls are involved. What happens after is a subject we do not broach.

○

Eager to feel like they were helping in some way, my incredible network of friends and family organized, through a national charity, to participate in a five-kilometre walk to raise money for leukemia research.

OCTOBER 20
6:30am, DL up for early start on RACE DAY!
8:20am, Mum arrives

A group of fifty or so marched, with babies, balloons, and dogs, behind a banner made with sheets and Sharpie that said, in block letters, HARRIET'S TEAM. It was a cool fall day, overcast, and the photos my dad took are grainy with the dusk. Everyone is smiling, even in the candid shots, looking beatific with hooded sweatshirts and pink cheeks as they march on the quiet weekend morning streets of Toronto.

After the walk, everyone made their way to the hospital, but I was too sick to see anyone. People had to wear gloves

and masks in order to even enter my room, and I was
sleeping more often than I was awake.

Eight storeys down, people gathered. There are photos of
my friends lying on the ground, the soles of their sneakers in
focus and their faces away from the camera, talking among
themselves. My drama teacher is in the foreground with his
four-year-old son, pointing to students, explaining to his child
what is happening. Then, from the other angle, there are faces
in focus, heads placed on stomachs, forming new shapes.
Knees bent, people pointing and looking up at my window.

There's one photo, taken from the ground, of the window
at the end of my hallway where I was sitting with my mum
and some nurses. It's eight floors up, so difficult to make out
the details, but I can see my mum with her bright, red-
lipsticked smile in the middle bay window, and the glint of
my IV pole next to her. She would have helped me put on
my slippers and push my IV, not holding my hand as
I wouldn't have wanted to be treated like an invalid. It was
my first time leaving my room in days. I only had the energy
to stay for a few minutes. When I had to leave, she would
have helped me lumber back to bed.

The gathering outside was captured in a series of
photographs by my mum from above, too, and from our
bird's-eye view, we could see what they were spelling with
their bodies: first HARRIET, then WE ♥ U, and then
everyone, all together, linked arms to form a giant, lumpy,
left-leaning and beautiful heart.

o

The bone marrow transplant had been encouraged by all
of the international researchers consulting on my case, but
as the infections in my body bore on, harder and harder,
opinions started to change.

As a consequence of my suppressed immune system,
I'd already had E. coli, Klebsiella, human torovirus, and
pneumonia. In addition to all that, the doctors gave
a potential diagnosis of Aspergillus as the cause for the
infection in my lungs and liver. Many of those things I'd
never heard of and didn't think about, so Aspergillus didn't
seem any different. But it was.

Aspergillus is a mould in the air we breathe: it's
everywhere all the time, like radio waves even if you don't
have the radio on. If this mould was in fact the cause of my
sickness, treatment would be an additional four to six weeks
and the bone marrow transplant would have to be put on
hold. In patients like me, the one-year survival rate with an
Aspergillus infection was less than 25 per cent.

My oxygen levels were dropping when I slept. I had to be put on a heart monitor and an oxygen sensor, and have tubes inserted up my nose.

> 12:15am, some rigors, more Demerol
> 1:15am, more rigors, more Demerol
> 2:15am, rigors, Demerol
> Watched the clock hands move mysteriously to fall back one hour
> 2:40am, rigors, Demerol
> Heart rate low, very sweaty.

My memories of this time are practically non-existent. My body was a machine, simply being told what to do. Just as I did then, I must rely on my parents and doctors. On the notes they took, on the memories they have.

oo

I am becoming too pregnant to still be living in the van. The plan is that once we make it to Vancouver I will go ahead and fly home, and Cal will drive back with the dogs. We spend our last night together next to a glacial lake in inland British Columbia, the water the colour of a blue popsicle, the sun warm as a heart. I wake up first, before Cal, before the dogs, with a lump in my throat. I watch, through the screen window next to our top-popped bed, as the sky lightens through the trees. Life will never be the same again, and I am so happy living in this endless state of becoming, in the optimism— albeit also the extreme, sometimes palpitating apprehension— that comes with waiting for something to happen. Soon, though, everyone else wakes up and the day starts happening, and I am living instead of worrying about living.

October 22: It has been a challenging time for Harriet recently, which is probably why I haven't posted an update. I find it easier when things are more upbeat. But you all need to know what Harriet is going through, and how you are continuing to help us all along this journey. Last Sunday was amazing—the walk for leukemia was an emotional time for us all. To see all those friends and family members below her hospital window was so uplifting. An incredible memory we shall treasure. The counts are not in for how much the walk raised, but we will let you know what a difference Harriet has made through the donations that were made in her honour—by people who know her, as well as many who don't but have heard her story.

Harriet's blood counts have been very low since this last round of chemo finished, resulting in high fevers and infections and so they have started to give her a new drug which stimulates white cell division so that she can help fight the bacteria in her body, as well as the barrage of antibiotics and antifungal treatments. With 2 peripheral IV's in her arms, she has to have daily visits from the "blood drawers" to test her counts as they can't do that through the IV's and the IVS have to be changed every 5 days, so there is lots of "poking" which is not nice. Harriet has not had her usual good appetite while she has been having high fevers, but that should return when the fevers subside and the counts start to rise again.

Please continue to hold Harriet in your thoughts and prayers. She is too weak to "hold court" just now, either on the phone or in her room, so notes in the mail or on her e-mail or website are great.

Fondly,

Mary

∞

When Fox was a puppy, I once left treats in his bowl for him to find upon coming back inside after peeing in the yard. Now, every time he comes into the house from the back door, he runs to his bowl to see if treats are there again.

This is how I think memory works. We might not remember the specific time something happened. But we remember remembering it the next day, and the day after that we remember the consequence of the memory. Memory becomes habit; it lives in our actions, in our bodies.

It took years until I wasn't afraid when I got a cold, or had a blood test. The memory of fear still lives in my body.

OO

When I passed the ten-year remission mark, at which point that Australian doctor said I had the same chance of getting cancer as anyone else, my dad told me that now my annual check-ups were about doing the medical system a favour. By continuing to show up and let the doctors note in their records that I am alive, I am letting the establishment know that it succeeded. That they did their job.

But now, home from my trip with Cal, I am eight and a half months pregnant and seeing doctors at least once a week to monitor my obstetrical health and the baby's development. I'm not only busy—my focus is shifting. This time, I decide to call and cancel my check-up.

O

The illness was still raging after twenty days of fever and I was getting worse.

From the progress reports:

Oct 22

Harriet continues to be greatly febrile.

Appetite down

x respiratory distress

x abdo pain

CT scan done tonight shows a significant worsening of both L+R upper lobes of lungs. In addition there is a lesion + lymphadenopathy, all new since scan from Oct 19

Significant worsening of pulmonary picture in face of continued poor clinical picture.

Oct 23

Clinical deterioration overnight.
Infectious Disease team to examine: pt is clinically worse.
Nurse note: Parents v. anxious. Many services in to see pt.

Oct 24

Nurse note: Harriet nervous + scared.

The doctors obtained permission from a drug company to administer a new drug prototype believed to work on Aspergillus, and they needed to move quickly.

○

My world was getting even narrower in focus.
My mum wrote in the journal:

Wed 30 Oct, 3:30pm, H walked to window
Thursday Oct 31, 1:40–2:30, Trick or Treating around 8A
with HL in wheelchair.

There's a photo of my mum and me standing in the hallway
outside my room. Pink pinwheel wallpaper, my name
written underneath the window, my chart in a slot next to
the door. My radiant mother is laughing at something off-
camera, and I can tell it's a real laugh since she has
a standard smile for photographs. She's wearing jewellery
and the red lipstick she always wore; I never once saw her
not looking put-together. I'm looking at the same thing she's
laughing at, but have an expression that's—I don't know,
actually. I look blank, somehow removed, observing with

detachment. My mouth is pursed; perhaps I was saying something. I'm wearing a rainbow clown wig with a white bandana underneath, because the cheap webbing of the wig was itchy. There's a triangle of my scalp visible: you can see a fuzzy darkening above my ears, and I still have most of my eyebrows. A little red circle has been painted on the tip of my nose, a stark contrast to my face, which is so pale it's reflective. I'm leaning on my IV pole with one hand; the other holds my four IV tubes and has an oxygen sensor attached at the index finger. There are two plastic hospital bracelets on my wrist: one white, the standard identification tag; and one red, an allergy tag to warn medical staff, in case I'm asleep or unconscious, of my allergies to certain medications. The knuckles on my hands are so defined, the strength and fragility of bone so exposed.

The bright flash means everything behind us is in darkness. Posy the clown is right behind me, her purple wig and purple tutu just visible between me and my shadow.

o

The drugs I was on: ciprofloxacin, meropenem, vancomycin, liposomal amphotericin B, caspofungin, voriconazole, fluconazole, ceftazidime, tobramycin, metronidazole, and GCSF. The bags of TPN also hung from my IV, and needed their own permanent tubing lines. The nurses encouraged me to get up as much as possible, to try to move around. If I continued to stay in bed all the time, I was at risk of sepsis.

Then, suddenly, the fever broke. One of my doctors used five exclamation marks when he wrote this in the progress report.

> Stable weekend. Afebrile x 24 hours!!!! Improved clinical situation!

The fever surged back briefly, then stayed at bay. I was recovering. They still did not know for sure what was causing the infection, but something was working.

Nov 4, 4:00pm, Dr. C said: No fever for 48 hours so cut
back on the antibiotics over weekend. Work on eating.
TPN being cycled off.

   Jen is the nurse tonight. Bath for H. Temp normal
at 9pm.

   Ready for bed (ie. sleep) at 9:30.

I love how my dad noted the distinction between bed and
sleep, since I was always in bed.

   After the weekend, a doctor came to say that based on
some recent ultrasounds, there might be a small clot in my
chest and possible lesions in my liver.

   My dad wrote on the forum:

No serious concern, but there may be some small lesions in
the liver, probably thought to be the same infection as in the
lungs. We knew a bit about that before. The Drs are thinking
about a possible opportunity to take a sample from the liver,
with a needle, and maybe also from the lungs. But no rush.
The Drs are consulting. Balancing the quest for a definitive
diagnosis against the risks involved, and considering the
alternative risks of prolonged treatment with drugs which
seem to be working (or at least helping), but which may be
a bit more aggressive than is really necessary.

A plan was being discussed for my release from the hospital
following this small procedure, presuming a sample would

be found, and the infection positively identified, so the appropriate drugs could be used to more specifically target whatever was causing it. I couldn't let myself trust this; I looked at it as if through a window.

○

Dr. L stopped by one afternoon. My parents weren't with me, and rather than wait for them, she just spoke with me. I was the target anyway. She wanted to tell me that while the discussion among the international specialists still had not reached a consensus, more of the group considered that, with the complications from my current infection, the risks of a transplant were too great. If my immune system was completely eradicated by the even-more-aggressive chemotherapy and full-body radiation required leading up to a bone marrow transplant, the Aspergillus would certainly flare up and smother me.

Another one of the rare moments my handwriting appeared in the notebook:

confirmed that transplant is off, not on hold.

My near-perfect match would still be in the bank, she reassured me, and ready in case I needed in later. This *later* already loomed large; I didn't need to be reminded.

I was not just disappointed—I was devastated. I didn't want a bone marrow transplant but I did want to live, and I had come to associate one with the other. This news made me more upset than my diagnosis had, because it felt as though the doctors were giving up on me.

My nurse from that shift wrote in the progress report:

Pt told by Dr. L that BMT is not to occur now a/t presumed fungal infection. Pt very upset + writer not in w/ pt at this time. Writer spoke with Dr. C who spoke w/ pt @ length regarding this decision. Harriet verbalized understanding. Dr. C also spoke w/ Mr. Lye on telephone after Harriet had called home upset.

○

Wednesday 6 Nov: 11:20am, Ivy disconnected!
  12:00, Escape. Freedom. To Kleinburg for lunch, then very
    brief visit to O's house. Back to 8A at 2:50pm.

I was released, my first time leaving the hospital since
September. In those two hours and fifty minutes the three
of us drove up to a farmhouse fifty kilometres outside of the
city where we had a lunch of soup and homemade bread
prepared by a woman I've known since I was born. There
was a clear plastic sheet over the white cotton tablecloth,
detailed with tiny pink roses. I've never liked butter but the
hospital nutritionist told me to try to eat as much fat as
I could, so I spread the cold butter in jagged chunks on the
fresh crumb of the soft white loaf. On the way home (*home*,
I write, when what I mean is the hospital) we visited my
great-aunt for what must have just been minutes, since we
had to get back for one of my IV antibiotics.

A few hours after we returned, the doctors came by to tell us that they might like to schedule what was described as a precautionary, minor, "no big problem" biopsy of my liver the following day.

∞

In bed one evening, I send my first friend from my university days in Halifax, who I haven't spoken with in a little while, a text that's just a red heart. She responds right away.

I was just thinking of you, and a conversation with you in 2005 where you were talking about motherhood.
    I felt so ambivalent about children at the time, but also that having a family was a certainty.
    You knew it was something amazing and worthwhile but did not see it as a certainty.

Oh wow. What a memory.
    Do you remember what I meant about having kids not being a certainty? That I wasn't sure I'd get the opportunity or didn't know if I wanted it?

(I don't remember ever not wanting children.)

Honestly, I think you were thinking of your health. So, opportunity.

I think the reason I remember is that you asked if I would think of naming a daughter Harriet. It stuck with me. Not in a morbid way.

I respond with the broken red heart.

So much love for you Harriet. And little 2005 Harriet.

O

The next day, I woke up from the biopsy in the intensive care unit. My liver had hemorrhaged. The liver is a giant bag of blood with millions of tiny blood vessels. It seems only logical that a needle, however thin, had broken it.

PICU Admission

This is a 15 ½ y/o F admitted to the PICU with acute bleed.
Abdo distended.
Pale.
Tearful, awake + responsive. Moving all 4 limbs.
Support + encourage parents.

Twelve blood transfusions were administered immediately, two new IVs were inserted, thick as straws, into each of my forearms, and one arterial line was put on the inside of my wrist so as to have constant read of my blood pressure.

Nurses finally had to draw blood from the veins in my feet to save space on my overtaxed arms.

My mum told me the doctors said, "We've lost her."

My dad doesn't remember it this way. "Didn't they just lose her blood pressure?"

"No blood pressure means you're dead," my mum says. "She had to be resuscitated. The doctors asked me if I wanted anyone there," my mum continues, "and I said the chaplain. He was at home in Thornhill and came down right away. It was nearly midnight."

Once he arrived, that tall gentle cowboy, my mum fainted. Her own blood pressure dropped. The nurses got her a room, and nearly sent her across the street to be admitted to the adult hospital.

"But they didn't?" I ask, filling in the gaps I missed.

"No, in the end they didn't," she says.

Once more, I felt like a seeing thing, not a living thing. I have a memory of seeing my whole body lying on a stretcher-bed in a bright white room. Was I dead? Is this a memory of the afterglow of me looking at my own body? Or did I just imagine this scene?

The surgeon who had performed the biopsy stayed nearby until one a.m., though his shift would have long been over. He showed us the needle that had been used for the biopsy: "It's thinner than a strand of hair," he said, pleadingly. The subtext: *please, you have to believe, this wasn't my fault.*

My dad's notes go all through the night. From 4:30 p.m. until eleven a.m., he was awake and monitoring me, noting morphine shots, blood pressure, oxygen levels, and the measurements taken of my abdomen, swollen and hard with blood. If they didn't get control of my blood pressure, if the internal bleeding didn't stop, I would be sent back into the operating room—with a dangerously low platelet count—for them to try to stitch up the leak.

One of my friends sat in the waiting room for two days. She wasn't allowed to come in: only immediate family were allowed in the ICU.

"Harriet doesn't have any siblings," my mum begged the hospital staff, "this is one of her best friends, the closest thing she has. Please."

In my moments of consciousness, I remember this friend sitting at my bedside and crying. I was so angry with her. "Keep that away from me," I said, though I'm not sure if I said it out loud. "*I'm* not crying."

At one point I tried to lift my waist up to have a bedpan inserted beneath me so that I could pee, and I fainted. A catheter was inserted, and the procedure had a pain I couldn't separate from embarrassment. I was even less in control of my own body now.

"Am I peeing?" I asked my dad.

He looked down at the bag hanging on the side of my bed-stretcher.

"No."

"How about now?"

He looked again. "Still no."

Some of my nurses from 8A came to visit me while I was in the ICU, and when they were on the other side of the curtain demarcating my space from the rest of the large room, I overheard them talking. One of them whispered, surely thinking I couldn't hear her, that I'd told her I had started thinking about dying, and when she said this, I thought: "Is that what I was talking about?"

I had recently asked her about some of the other patients on the ward who had died, and we'd talked about my reliance on sleeping pills and how, now weaning, I realized I never wanted to sleep, but wanted to be alive as much as possible. Was I talking about dying then? Now that she'd said it, I supposed I had been.

In reading this section of the journals I become very aware that they could have ended. It could have been over at any point, but life, and the writing of it, feels especially fragile and urgent in these pages. And then, what would an end have looked like? What would my parents have written? Time of death? Would that have been the end?

Heracles said: "Alcestis lay dead."

The servant responded: "And all of us died with her."

∞

I can't say I ever believed in heaven, though I've wanted to. What I can say is that I agree with all the scientists and poets who, in their wisdom, point to how, in nature, nothing truly dies. The energy in all things must become a different kind of energy. Though everything living must die, their parts become something else. That's a kind of continuance. (Are children another kind of continuance?) I have to believe this; I have to believe something. Put my body in the ground and plant a rosebush on top. My body will become worms, then roses, then birds. My body will be endlessly becoming.

The Hospital for Sick Children
Department of Psychology

Telephone Consultation
Patient: Harriet Lye

Purpose of session:
Ms. C telephoned Mrs. Lye to inquire about Harriet's well being and coping with treatment.

Mrs. Lye indicated that the entire family is at a low point right now because Harriet is experiencing complications after finishing her last cycle of chemotherapy. Mrs. Lye also informed me that Harriet has told her for the very first time that she feels that she is "losing the battle." Mrs. Lye indicated that she told Harriet that she needs to keep on believing in her strength. She also told her daughter that she is at a low point right now but that this will pass. I told Mrs. Lye that it was very powerful when she told Dr. B and myself during our last interview that a massage therapist who was working with Harriet told her that he had never felt a stronger and more vibrant spirit in a weak body. Mrs. Lye thanked me for reminding her about that. She also told me that she is very spiritual and prays in Harriet's room but she does not know if Harriet prays as well. She also added that she does not feel comfortable asking Harriet about praying because her daughter is a very private person.

Mrs. Lye sounded more uplifted when she told me about a run/walk for cancer. Mrs. Lye informed me that forty-nine people showed up (and a dog) and they formed a heart on the street in front of Harriet's window. Mom said that Harriet looked out the window and when she disappeared, the students became very emotional.

Summary,

Mrs. Lye seemed upset during the majority of the telephone consultation and her tone of voice sounded a lot lower than in previous conversations. She seemed more cheerful when she talked about Harriet's friends forming a human heart outside Harriet's hospital window.

Sincerely,

P. K. C., M.A.

Department of Psychology

○

In the ICU, the only sustenance that passed my lips for days was ice chips. Then we were told I needed to stop eating even the ice chips: enclosed in an ileus of blood, my gut was unable to digest anything, including water. I threw it all up. My mum made a list in the margins of the notebook of the food I wanted once I was allowed to eat again.

HARRIET WANTS TO EAT:

Rainbow sherbet

Creme soda

Apple juice

Clementines

Red peppers and Caesar dip

Frozen blueberries

HARRIET WANTS TO SEE:

Home

○○

The van is the first home Cal and I built together, with its fairy lights and solar panels, but as we drive around the country, we make pit stops at the house in Toronto we are making into our home. Cal has lived here for almost eight years, with many different stages of roommates, sometimes as many as six people at once, in what one friend called "the hipster mansion."

The house belongs to Cal's aunt, whose late partner grew up in it and left it to her. The uncle's mother and father, who would have bought the house when they married sixty years ago, are long dead, but we still receive mail for them from Polish churches.

It's a giant, crumbling, poorly insulated manor of a house in a part of town that neither of us could ever afford to live in normally. Cal's old bedroom was the attic and the heat doesn't reach that far up, so in the cold months he'd sleep in a hat and sleeping bag, and in the coldest months, when the temperature went below minus twenty, he'd sleep on the couch downstairs.

Over the summer, the roommates move into their new homes and help me move my things in. Neighbours, noticing my belly, start to bring us hand-me-down clothes, old strollers, rocking horses, pictures their kids have drawn for us, and Tupperwares of chili.

Whenever we are home during that hot summer, we make what feel like weekly trips to the paint store at the top of the street, and daily trips to the lake at the bottom. Every room ends up a different shade of white, Cal painting every one of them by himself as I read or nap or walk the dogs. We have many serious, considered conversations about which shade of white each room should be, and he finally confesses: "Harriet. I can't tell the difference between Cotton Balls and Chantilly Lace."

It's funny to think that everything we're doing now is for the baby. Perhaps that's not funny at all, but rather the most normal thing. Everything in our worlds now orbits around this. I find it peaceful to have such a singular purpose.

I once told a therapist that my greatest fear was becoming homeless, and he helped me figure out that this was actually about survival. My life fell apart once and I lived through it, and I'm afraid it will happen again and I won't. A house represents your soul, your self, and not having one represents a fundamental insecurity.

When I move into this house, though it's owned by family—a family that I am now coming to accept is, through my great fortune, *my* family—I still fear the same things, perhaps more so. The more you have, the more you can lose.

○

At 11:55 a.m. on November 8, a doctor from Infectious Diseases came to tell us that nothing was growing yet from the biopsy of my liver. My dad noted later, beside it: *still may be able to tell what it was.* My fever was already coming back, the blood inside my body was still pooling where it shouldn't be, and my dad was refusing to give up hope that all of this hadn't been for nothing.

Days later, the biopsy revealed that the lesions "seemed to be natural fatty deposits." A crack appeared in my faith in the medical system.

OO

I've had a feeling I would give birth two days early, and on this morning, this beautiful and bright fall morning, my contractions start, gentle and purposeful. I walk to the lake and write the baby a letter.

Swans are feeding in the shallows, upside down with their faces and long necks invisible, but I know they are there. At what point does history allow us to use conjecture to fill in the gaps? At what point can I see a swan's body and tail feathers sticking up in the water and trust that there is a swan's long neck and orange beak on the other side?

"I don't think I can know now how much I will love you," I write. "I'm only just letting myself start to dip my feet into the water, but I already know how deep it is."

November 16: It's been a long time since I wrote an update, so here I go! It has been a challenging time for us since the liver biopsy of November 7. We were all in such a state of shock afterwards and needed to focus all our energies (already depleted) on Harriet. Her body is still trying to deal with the physical loss of blood from her liver that formed an ileus around her bowel, putting it into paralysis, as well as the emotional trauma of being so close to going home and rebuilding her life and then being completely turned around — intensive care, immobility, heavy duty narcotics for pain, etc. The progress is slow as her body deals with reabsorbing the ileus and she tries to get up a little more each day.

My cousin came down to stay with Harriet last night for two hours so that David and I could go outside the hospital for dinner. That felt so strange, the two of us together, and neither of us with Harriet.

Fondly,

Mary

OO

The baby, we name him Arlo, is born swiftly, smoothly,
a perfect and healthy baby. I have no drugs or interventions
or tearing of the flesh. A nurse tells me my body was made to
have babies. I smile at what she means to be a compliment
and think about how, if this can be said to be true, my body
hadn't known that.

When he is out on this side of my body, the doctors ask if
I want to hold him first or have him examined. The
examination should only take a few minutes, they say, and
will happen right there in the room with me.

"Examine him," I say instantly.

I didn't trust my body during pregnancy because I have
known its betrayal. My body had created its own death and,
despite all the tests that proved otherwise, I still could not
believe that it could create a perfect, untarnished life.

I couldn't let myself fall in love with my baby before
I knew it was safe.

O

On November 23, for the first time in seven weeks, I was allowed home. The nurses gave me a shot of morphine for the road and then we were there, home, all together, for a whole afternoon.

That day, my dad's hand:

12:30pm, Harriet singing in the shower.
1:30pm, free! Home!

I had been feverless for long enough and had just been taken off the liquid iv food. The pain in my back for which I was taking morphine was, everyone hoped, manageable with Tylenol.

7:50pm, back to 8A. No need for Ivy until 9am for
    Caspofungin but best to hook it up early in case of need
    for morphine.

9:30, 37.4 C
10:50, Ivy hooked up again
11:30pm, morphine and Imovane
5:30am, morphine
9:30am, more morphine

The plan for the rest of the weekend was to get me ready for discharge on Monday. My mum noted that on Sunday we went to the mall together, had Swiss Chalet for dinner, then were back at the hospital "for the last night."

Monday I was discharged. It felt very anticlimactic: I didn't believe the cord had really been cut. Sure enough, Tuesday morning I had a fever, my dad called the doctors, and they told us to come in.

It was always my dad who drove me into Emergency, always late at night when the fevers spiked, always rolling down the winding highway that had been carved through the Don Valley, following the river. The dynamic felt Greek: my father and I heading to war, my mother, a Penelope, stoking the home fires.

H & D at emerg 2:10am, 38.9 C, 49.8kg
blood taken, urine sample, chest X-ray at 3:20am
4:45am Ivy hooked up.

Wednesday discharge, back home; Thursday a new fever, back to the hospital.

H & D at emerg 1:30am, 39.9 C, 48.5kg
10:05am ultrasound, cheerios.
Dr. G. 1pm, morphine. Antibiotics starting.

The nurses were trying to keep me off the IV food; if
I became dependent on this it would be all the more
difficult to leave. The things I ate over the next two days:
popcorn, an apple, juice, pretzels, more popcorn, more
juice, another apple. I didn't keep much of it down. On the
third day, the IV food was hooked up.

Monday was my mum's birthday. My dad wrote:

9:30am, called Mary on her new cellphone to sing Happy
Birthday.

My mum wrote:

1pm, walk, playing Scattergories, much laughter.
2:45pm, Dr. H examines H. Better than yesterday.
* Ask Drs tomorrow if magnesium thru IV at home.
Lots of techno features on new phone!

My parents went out for an hour and a half to have pizza by
themselves, and I was with my nurses. I watched while Jenna
made my mum a birthday hat out of a large plastic cup,
using a rubber tourniquet for a chinstrap and some tape to
make a bow on top. The nurses had planned a birthday

surprise for her, all coming to sing "Happy Birthday" at the shift change at seven p.m. so both the morning and night nurses could be there.

There's a photograph of my parents flanking me as I lie in my cot, my hair all fallen out but my head already fuzzy with new growth, all of us smiling so hugely, my mum holding the cup-hat to her head, and I think now: Isn't it remarkable how and where we are able to find joy?

OO

Safe. He's safe.

I know it isn't biologically true, but looking at my baby in the minutes, hours, days after he's born, I feel as though I'm looking at a representation, or manifestation, of my own interiority. An emissary from the invisible.

The vernix, the ashy, waxy white coating he's born with, is still on the insides of his butter-soft arms, behind his knees, in the folds of his neck and hips. That's from inside of me. But then, so is all of him. And if he's some kind of reflection of the state of myself, I feel a compound relief: we are both perfect. I feel a purity I've never felt before. In the rules that I've invented, Arlo is evidence that everything is just fine.

Did you know, actually, that growing a baby in your body can heal some of the small broken parts? Stem cells migrate across the blood barrier of the placenta and target sites of injury. The cells live in the mother's body for decades.

○

After repeated ultrasounds and X-rays of my back, the
doctors of the infectious diseases department determined
that the pain I was feeling in my ribs, a pain so bad I needed
regular morphine, even though I hated the feeling it gave me,
was a pleural effusion, something that sounds not at all like
what it is. I knew effusions to be some kind of unrestrained
heartfelt outburst, but medically they are an escape of fluid
into a body cavity—in this case, the lining of the lung.

There was a thought to intervene and drain it, my dad
wrote, *but it is best left alone—there is little to gain by
draining it.* This time, having seen what had happened
before, the doctors decided that the intervention risked
causing further damage, outweighing its possible benefits.

On December 6, there's a photo of six of my nurses
standing grinning around my bed, my dad standing behind
them in the doorway. No bags are hanging from my IV, the
grey cord and plug looped around its neck, ready to find a

new owner; and a gift bag with yellow smiley faces and pink tissue paper is on the bed in front of me. A goodbye present from the nurses. I'm wearing my short wig and looking away from the camera, happy.

The doctors said I could continue medications at home, my dad newly trained by a home care nurse to give me my daily infusions of the Aspergillus medication I would need for up to six months. The plan was that I would come to clinic every week, then every month, then every three months, then six, then twelve. I would have been happy to go back every day forever, so long as it would mean I would be safe.

But after that, I never had another night in the hospital. There were no more fevers, no more complications, no more treatment, no relapses. At first things were tentative. The journal continued day by day, always written by my dad, as he performed my infusions every evening, and as he continued to bring me to my check-ups and medical procedures and blood tests.

For the first weeks, all my visitors were still noted— friends, family, the home care nurse—as well as the places I went. The mall, the movies, a friend's house. He'd take my temperature every night and note whether I had nausea, but also, because it was a novelty, he would note if nothing happened. *Quiet day*, he'd write, I imagine with such pleasure, with a profound new enjoyment of quietness. When you're living it, you never know when something will be the end. This could just as easily have been another one of the interludes, in between fevers or other complications.

I was like an astronaut who had become used to the rhythms and constraints of living in my little space station, and now I was cut loose in the darkness, the vastness, of eternity.

∞

We bring Arlo home in the early morning. I say early, but it was really more like ten or eleven a.m. I hadn't slept in three days, though, and because it was overcast—the sun hadn't emerged that day from behind the duvet of clouds—time felt softer than ever. It was early in that it was a new beginning. The reason for our home had arrived.

We made this house for you, I think, as we carry our baby through to the kitchen.

The light is grey but bright, like day-old snow. I get the good camera from the back room and take a picture of Cal sitting at the table he built, holding Arlo, so small, asleep, in a grey woollen jumpsuit that's far too big for him because I just didn't believe babies could be as small as everyone said they were. Arlo's cheeks are round pink apples and his ears have been copy-pasted from my own. His eyes are still puffed closed from the labour of his journey here (they'll only be open for a few minutes this whole week). And his mouth, his perfect raspberry-pink mouth, and those fingernails, so small and still so perfect.

With his right index finger, Cal is holding Arlo's whole hand, and this meeting point is in the centre of the photograph. Even in sleep, Arlo's grip is strong: you can see the creases in his tiny fingers as he holds on tight. The dogs are both looking intently at these hands, too: Disco's black head is cocked to the side right beneath Cal, and Fox is keeping at a slight distance, by the window, but his head leans in, curious.

This, right here, has become the narrow and expansive focus of my whole world.

That night I have a bath by myself—my first time by myself, truly, in forty weeks. I think it will feel significant, but it doesn't really. The baby isn't something I'm desperate to be away from. In fact, I want to be near him always.

Getting out of the bath, I rub lotion onto my calves, my shoulders, my belly, holding for a moment there, feeling the stretch of skin. Candles in the bathroom light up the night, though I have no idea what kind of night it's like out there, and won't for days. What's inside the house is all that matters to me right now. Absentmindedly rubbing my newly empty belly and looking out the window, thinking of my love and my baby sleeping in the bedroom, I say, very quietly, "Thank you, house."

January 23, 11:50 p.m., 2003

It has been cold enough this winter (as usual) to make the outdoor skating rink in Tannery Park behind our house.

(I haven't been out flooding yet this winter, other people have been looking after it so far this year.)

Anyway, Harriet and her friend P. decided to go out for a skate this evening, about 9:30 pm. Very clear and cold, about -15C maybe, and lots of stars out. Orion & the big dipper easily spotted, with Polaris. I went out with them, but not on skates this time.

It was deserted for some reason, and the ice was pretty good. So the girls had a good skate around for maybe 15 or 20 minutes, but we all came in again before frostbite set in. Harriet looked great.

That's all.

Not much other news really.

David

This was the last post in the forum.

OO

The three of us, our new family, on a drive together. Arlo is three days old. The leaves in the forest are pale yellow, pre-gold. Looking out the window I see two old men driving in a burgundy sedan and I burst into tears, my whole face instantly wet.

"What's wrong?" Cal asks.

"One day, Arlo will be old and we'll be dead and we won't know how he's doing," I say, sobbing inconsolably, aware again of this asymmetry of the love of a child and the love of a parent, and it makes me sob even harder thinking that, once he's an old man, though I trust he will mourn our loss, he will—I hope he will—reach a point where he won't even mind that we're not there to call him up and ask how he's doing.

Cal laughs, reaches for my hand, and I look up from our baby. In this moment, I am alive, and he is alive, and Cal says "yes," smiling at us both, "that's the goal."

THANKS TO: My family—the one I came from and the one I made. My friends—from then, now, and always. The nurses, doctors, and staff at The Hospital for Sick Children. For reading early drafts: Katharine Campbell, Laura Dawe, Michelle Engel, Caroline Schuurman, Lucy André, my dad. For believing in this book and giving it a place in the world: Stephanie Sinclair, Jared Bland. Melanie Little, for the important details. Editors at VICE and the *Globe & Mail* who published some of these stories in essays: Jennifer Schaffer, Arielle Pardes, Catherine Dawson March. The Toronto Arts Council, the Ontario Arts Council, and the Canada Council for the Arts, who all supported this book, affording me more time to work and the confidence I often needed to continue. And thanks to you, for reading.